A LENGTHY LIST
OF LOVERS

Kira Rice-Christianson

For Tony. My sweet and sensitive lover. You have inspired me in every way. You have showed me a love that is not rooted with ownership. You have instilled in me a sense of reality, and a desire to learn and grow. Thank you for reminding me of the importance to actively participate in life, and to never follow someone else's rules. I will love you forever. The woman I am becoming is capable of anything, and you are a part of her.

To me, love has always meant purpose. It is the one thing that gives meaning to all things. It inspires us. It breaks us down to the core of our existence, and we are reborn with a fresh pair of hands to touch another. It turns mundane routines into unforgettable moments. Love is the one universal craving, it feeds us for a lifetime. I realize this is a bit of a hopeless romantics perspective, and I suspect we are a dying breed. One thing I know for sure, is I have had many lovers, and they have all left me with something. The good, the bad, and the ugly; it's all etched into me, like if you shake my body you'll see them on my skin. More importantly, each and every one of them played a major role in my greatest discovery; the only eternal love of my life, myself. With every lost lover I became closer to my independence. I suppose I could thank them for that. I have loved men, I have loved women. I have lost innocence, I have found freedom. I have stories to tell, secrets to share, wounds to lick. I'm not here to drop every name, or dish every dirty detail, but rather to share experiences; experiences that, as I look back, I understand have changed me. So here it is, my lengthy list of lovers. From the casual crushes to the messy heartbreaks. I suppose if this gets out, there will be plenty of bruised egos in my email. (Most of the names in these stories have been altered in attempt to respect their privacy. Enjoy.)

Volume I

Tory

As a child, I was very eager for male attention. Not only attention, but approval. I did just about everything to prove to the boys that I was pretty and cool. I stuffed my bra with toilet paper and pretended to care about kickball at recess. I fabricated stories that made my life sound way too interesting for a young girl. I stole lipstick and perfume from my mom. I was quick to pick up on the things that boys liked, and I was quick to practice them.

It started as early as kindergarten, shortly after my dad left. I'm no psychologist, but I'm sure there is a correlation there. In fact, I believe my relationship with my father has had a hefty impact on my love life. Go figure. I find similarities in the types of men I have chased, and the insecurities I have developed. As I look back, it is very clear that I was attempting to fill a space. I'll go deeper into this at some point, but for now, let's keep it light.

I used to chase little boys around the playground, singing in the most taunting tone, "I'm gonna kiiiiiss yooooooou. I'm gonna kiiiiiss yooooou." One day, I chased my crush of the week down the slides and around the jungle gym, threatening to plant his cheek with a wet kiss. He must have been terrified of catching cooties, because he ran so fast that he fell and cracked his head open. Instead of getting a kiss, he got a ride to the hospital and stitches in his skull. I swear, men will do anything to avoid commitment.

As the years of elementary school went on, I went through several innocent crushes like this. The older I got, the more interested I was in calling someone my boyfriend. I realize that elementary may seem a little early for these kinds of thoughts, but in my youth, it was never vulgar. My hopes were wholesome. I only wanted a boy to hold my hand and give me compliments. Maybe even give me my first kiss.

In 5th grade, I met Tory. Tory was a new student from Texas. We lived in rural Illinois, so his southern speech was exciting to me. He was tall, with long and skinny limbs that hung awkwardly when he walked. He had braids that hung at the middle of his neck and were tied off with red and white beads. His eyes were mature, a dark brown, always surrounded with dark circles. He wasn't the cutest boy I'd seen, but something about him caught my attention. Within 2 weeks of knowing him, he was my boyfriend, and we were obsessed with each other.

Tory and I would pass notes to each other everyday. We talked about our plans to get married, have 2 kids and move to a big house on the beach by the time we were 25. I still laugh at my idea of adulthood back then. We sat next to each other at lunch, and we hung out under the big oak tree at recess. He walked me home from school and called me as soon as he got home. I had butterflies in my stomach everytime I saw him, heard him, even thought about him.

One day, while walking me home from school, Tory stopped and said

"I think we should kiss."

I remember letting go of his hand because I was embarrassed of how sweaty my palms had become. I was nervous, but I agreed. I leaned in, standing on my tippy-toes, and I let him kiss me. It was a simple, clumsy, close-mouthed peck, but let me tell you, 10-year-old me thought I was in love. We went on like this for a few weeks. I doodled his name in my notebooks and he flirted with me from across the classroom. We were inseparable.

Parent teacher conferences were coming up, and unlike some of the other kids, I wasn't worried. I participated in class, did well on every assignment, and stayed out of trouble. I wasn't a bad kid, or at least that's what I thought. To my surprise, my teacher had a different opinion. I sat next to my mom, across from my teachers desk, expecting to hear about my accomplishments. Instead, Mrs.Gwell paused before speaking with pressed lips, and then said

"Your daughter has been very inappropriate with one of the boys in this class. They were caught passing notes about very adult things, including sex."

My jaw dropped.

"*SEX?*" I thought.

It wasn't true. My face went red and I wanted to cry. She was lying. I looked over at my mom, whose eyebrows were raised to the top of her head in a sort of angered shock. I could not believe that a teacher would lie to a mother about a child. I did not understand why she would invent false stories about me and Tory. We never talked about sex, I wasn't even thinking about it.

I sat there, frozen, trying to swallow the lump in my throat. I was remarkably embarrassed and noticeably confused. But I had nothing to say. I was afraid.

My mother had me when she was very young, 16 to be exact. She was always the youngest parent among her peers, which I believe she caught plenty of slack for. I think the idea of me feeding into what everyone already thought of us really upset her. Once we got home, I spent the entire night pleading with her, begging her to believe me. I remember the crocodile tears that drenched my face and the collar of my shirt. Whether she believed me or not, it was too late. She grounded me and told me I was too young for a boyfriend.

At that point, Mrs.Gwell was already responsible for stripping the first bit of my innocence. I'm still not certain why she did it. I have my theories, one being that she had an issue with interracial dating. Maybe a white girl dating a black boy made her blood boil enough to make up rumors about children. As an adult I can look back on these moments with a little more insight and attempt to understand why things happened the way they did. However, this particular situation still leaves me pretty lost.

Somehow, word spread quickly, like it always does in my hometown. And at age 10, I was tainted. I was no longer the sweet and curious girl. I was the fast girl, the girl who was trying too hard to grow up too quickly, the girl who everyone assumed would get knocked up early. That image stayed with me for the rest of my school days. I wore it like a scarlet letter until it became a part of my personality. The older I got, the more unapologetic I became.

But I'll never forget how humiliating it was in the beginning. Despite the fact that the things people said about me were untrue, I was ashamed. I was too young to feel dirty in that way. I ended things with Tory, and walked myself home the next day.

Volume II

Candace

I learned pretty early in life that if you do not adapt, you will be crushed. So once everyone had decided that I was the designated school slut, I did just that; I adapted. I may not have known anything about sex, love, or relationships, but I was going to pretend like I did. I was going to fake it until I could make it, and yes, I did a lot of faking it.

Throughout middle school, I had several boyfriends. Most of them didn't last more than a month. Although, I remember a couple of them had me staring at pictures in my room with the door locked, listening to Rascal Flatts and crying my 12 year old eyes out. However, it never took me more than a week to bounce back.

I became obsessed with the attention that boys gave me. My life revolved around it. I'd sneak in moments between school and home to make googly eyes at my boyfriend of the month, and hold hands by the big green hill next to the school. My idea of fun was pretending to be in love.

The older I got, the more serious my relationships started to feel. 8th grade specifically was a pivotal time for me. I had my first identity crisis as soon as I turned 13. The hormones in my body were on fire and I was discovering so many emotions for the first time. I started listening to some really strange alternative rock, dying my hair black and hanging out with other people who hated their lives. I was coming into a very hardcore rebellious stage. In fact, I ended up getting caught shoplifting, expelled from school, and grounded for the entire Summer that year. I really went all out.

At this point in my life, things weren't the greatest at home. I won't go too into detail, because the purpose of this book is not to share my life story, but I will say that my mother and I had a complicated relationship. The friend group I had acquired were probably not the best influences, but they were the only people who I felt truly understood me. There were four girls, and one guy. One of the girls was my age, but everybody else was a year older; which made them freshmen in high school. I looked up to them. Every weekend we would all get together and see what kind of shit we could stir up.

One member of our little crew was Candace. Candace was a short and skinny Vietnamese girl with frail black hair and a bit of an androgynous thing going on. We would always go to her house to hang out. Her room was one of those bonus rooms in the upstairs of her dads house, and her dad was never home. In other words, we had space and we had privacy.

Candace showed an interest in me very shortly after we became friends. I had never been with a girl, but I knew I was attracted to them, and I was definitely attracted to Candace. She was so cute, and impossible not to be drawn to. She wasn't necessarily aggressive, but she certainly wasn't shy. She was the initiator of the relationship, being the first to admit her feelings.

It was new years eve, and our group plus a couple more were hanging out at Candace's house. Her dad was gone, and we managed to get our hands on a bottle of UV vodka. I think Candace's older sister bought it for us. It was my second time ever drinking, and it never even crossed my mind that I was too young to be experiencing things like this, I always felt older than I was. We were all listening to music and having a good time, when Candace pulled me to the side to talk.

"I think I want to be with you." She said to me, very directly. We sat on the staircase, side by side.

"What about Elle?" I asked.

Elle was her ex-girlfriend, who sometimes hung out with us. I was under the impression that Candace wanted to get back with her.

"She will probably be crushed, but I don't care anymore.
I want to be with you."

I started to tingle all over and the liquid courage spilled
out of me. I leaned in to kiss Candace, and that was my
answer. She was my girlfriend, and I was on top of the
world; an entirely new world for me.

Candace had this way about her, she made
everyone in her life feel important. She was sort of the
leader of our little group, so I felt particularly special
being her girlfriend. We broke the news to our friends
and continued to celebrate the rest of the night. I was
elated. It was all so fast and exciting. It was my first time
being with a girl, and how lucky I was to be with one of
the most interesting girls I had ever met.

When the word got out at my school, people had
plenty of questions. I had never officially come out as
bisexual, and as I mentioned previously, I had several
boyfriends prior to Candace. People were shocked to say
the least. I don't remember anyone being cruel to me,
but it was clear that certain people kept their distance. A
couple of people that I considered close friends started
talking to me less, and the preppy crowd gave me
halfway sympathetic glances in the halls. Everyday I
answered questions like

"So, you're a lesbian now?"

"You don't like guys anymore?"

"Have you had sex? How do you even have sex with a girl?"

At first I didn't mind answering their questions, and ignoring their confused stares. But it got old, fast. A lot of people would ask me how my parents reacted, but actually, I never told my mom. As far as she was concerned, nothing had changed, Candace was still my best friend. I think later on she had her suspicions, and eventually put two-and-two together, but she never really talked to me about it. I preferred it that way, it wasn't a conversation I was dying to have. It's not that I was afraid my mom would judge me, she was young and open-minded. Mainly, I didn't want her to start restricting how often I saw Candace or whether or not I could stay the night at her house.

I didn't want anything getting in the middle of my relationship with Candace. I loved being around her. She had so many friends, and she was good to all of them. We mostly continued to hang out as a group, so I really had to fight for her attention, but it was always so rewarding when I got it. I loved kissing her. That's all we ever did, really. Although emotionally I was deeply involved, physically our relationship stayed fairly innocent.

Candace went on tugging my heart around for a few months. After a while, it began to feel like I was constantly chasing her, working to keep her happy and entertained. Eventually it just felt like I wasn't enough for her. However, this didn't make me want her any less. In fact, quite the opposite. I so desperately wanted to hang onto her.

That Summer, after managing to get myself into all of the trouble that I mentioned previously, I was *so* grounded. I'm talking no phone, no internet, no communication to the outside world grounded. I was permitted to watch TV and think about my actions for the entire Summer. As you could imagine, this put a pretty hefty damper on my relationship. I tried my best to sneak in computer time when my mom was at work, being careful to erase the history when I was finished. I tried to message Candace, explaining to her what had happened. I wrote her novels, telling her that I loved her and I wouldn't be able to see her for a couple of months. I asked her to wait for me, as if I was going to prison for 25 to life. It was dramatic, but it felt very real at the time. I never got a response. I remember writing her name on the wall behind my bed in permanent marker while daydreaming about seeing her again.

A couple of weeks into my grounding sentence, Candace showed up at my doorstep. My mothers boyfriend was home, and he answered the door. He asked her to leave, and explained that I was not allowed to talk to anyone that wasn't family. I listened to the conversation from my bedroom, and as soon as I heard the door shut I rushed to my window. I was able to wave Candace down, and my heart raced as she walked over to me.

I don't recall the conversation word for word. I only remember one part really, and I remember how I felt after. Candace informed me that she was working on things with her ex, and they were getting back together. She said she was sorry, and she would talk to me soon. I knew that was a lie, seeing how I was grounded and the only way she managed to break this news to me was by somehow hitching a ride all the way out to my neighborhood (which was across town from hers.) She came with two of our friends. I couldn't help but think that this made them more of her friends than they were mine. I couldn't help but think that not only was I losing my girlfriend, but my entire group. Then I thought, how long did they know? How long were they scheming behind my back, contemplating how and when they would tell me? How long were they letting me live in a fantasy world? I wondered if things would be different if I never got in trouble, or if they would have run their course either way.

In hindsight, I think this was my first experience
with betrayal. This was the first moment I felt that the
world that I was living in was crumbling to pieces around
me. Sure, today I don't flinch in the slightest talking
about it. Over ten years have passed, and I can admit
that teenage me was a bit dramatic. But at that moment,
I was hurt, heartbroken even. All of that adapting, all of
that pretending, suddenly it was real life.

Can you remember your first heartbreak?
However silly it may seem looking back, can you
remember the feeling in that moment? Did your heart
skip a beat, or did it multiply? Did your palms sweat,
your mouth get dry? It felt like all of the above for me.
Maybe it was the new, racing hormones in my body that
heightened it, because it felt like something I could never
recover from. It felt like the end of the world. It hurt so
bad that I placed both hands on my chest in hopes to
hold it together. I spent the rest of my punishment
crying over her.

As time passed, I started hanging out with some
of my older friends that I had neglected. I started dating
boys who felt disposable, again. It wasn't that I was no
longer interested in girls, honestly there just weren't that
many openly gay girls in my hometown. Later in life, I
had a few runs with a few women who really weren't that
different from Candace. It became clear that I am
attracted to magnetic women that are likely to break my
heart. Anyways, I licked my wounds and eventually got
over her. Years later we ran into each other at a local bar

and had one of those halfway awkward, halfway intriguing conversations. She didn't seem different at all, she still had the same intense energy. I even caught myself flirting with her a bit. She told me I looked good, I smiled and imagined the little girl she probably remembered me as. I certainly was not her, anymore.

To this day, I am surprisingly thankful for my relationship with Candace. Sure, she introduced me to things I was definitely too young for, things like weed and alcohol. Sure, she ditched me for her ex the moment that being with me became inconvenient. But she was my first girlfriend, and she taught me to always be completely unapologetic about who I loved. She showed me what it meant to love such a strong personality, which I imagine is how some people who have been with me felt. Most importantly, I learned that even when it feels like i've lost everything, I can still pick up what's left and move forward. I learned many things about myself by being with Candace, how could I not be grateful for that?

Volume III

Calen

Shortly after the end of my first relationship with a girl, I decided to stay away from them for a while. Candace broke my heart, and I carried that energy with me. As far as I was concerned, girls were smarter, and sneakier. You can hardly tell when they are lying. They will stop loving you way before they decide to let you know, and you probably won't have a clue that it's coming. As amazing and magical as they are, they scared me. At this point, my reputation was completely tarnished, so I could pretty much do whatever I wanted and nobody would be surprised. With that being said, I resumed my pattern of hopping from boy to boy. Whoever would give me attention, and wasn't a complete creep was eligible in my book.

Then came Calen.

I had just started high school and Calen was new to the district. He had transferred from the town over, so I had never seen him before. He was the definition of tall, dark, and handsome, and his nonchalant attitude was my biggest weakness. Calen was good at two things; playing basketball and getting girls. Every girl wanted their chance with Calen, even most of my friends. Sorry for them, I reached him first. I was an experienced dater by age 14, so I had no problem walking straight up to him and expressing my interest.

As it turned out, we lived in the same neighborhood. We started walking home together most days, when he didn't have basketball practice. I don't remember ever having relevant conversations. I mainly did a lot of childish giggling while he pulled me closer to him. He teased me a lot. He was pretty insulting, actually. He would say things like,

"Your crooked teeth ass," or "Damn girl, you so thirsty."

I would roll my eyes and push him away, and he would say something like

"I'm just fuckin with you." then kiss me on the cheek or the forehead.

As much as he mocked me, I questioned if he liked me at all. I told myself he must if he was spending time with me. I didn't consider the possibility of being used. There was no way to be sure, but I was willing to take that risk. I wanted him, anyway.

It didn't take long for word to get out that we were an item, despite the fact that we never actually had that conversation. Everyone at school knew that we were seeing each other. If they didn't catch a glimpse of us flirting in the halls between classes, I made it clear that he was off-limits when they asked. As far as I was concerned, he was mine. He may not have agreed, he may not have always acted as such, but I had my own versions of reality.

So here I was, completely obsessed, and possibly delusional. I was willing to do just about anything for this boy who probably didn't even know my middle name. I did anything and everything to get him to like me, including putting myself in various questionable situations. I lied to my mom on multiple occasions, telling her that I was staying after school to get help on a project when really I'd be sneaking around with Calen. Usually we would hang out around the park, just off of school grounds. On rare occasions, we would go to his house when his mom was working. Like I said, questionable situations.

As a 14 year old girl, I wasn't necessarily advanced sexually. I had made it to first base, mostly kissing and limited touching. I was virgin territory, for sure. (If you're reading this mom, I'm sorry, you did great.) Looking back, I think this may have been one of the main, or only reasons Calen showed any type of interest in me. It makes sense, considering my far from innocent reputation. I was probably considered an easy target for the horny high school boys. I remember his friends would always ask me

"Have you let him hit yet?"

I would scoff and tell them to mind their business. They would laugh every time, shake hands and say something like "my boy." I was secretly a little flattered. I felt good about myself knowing that boys thought of me in a sexual way. How naive I was. If only I had known back then, most boys will fuck anything with a pulse, I wouldn't have been so foolish. I started to feel like if I wanted Calen to have the same feelings that I had, I had to step my game up. I had to be the type of girl that he wanted, the type of girl that everyone already assumed I was, and that type of girl is willing to put out.

One day after school, I found myself at Calen's house. We sat on his brown leather couch and started kissing. He was an OK kisser, but I'm sure I wasn't much better. After what seemed like barely a minute, he took his shirt off. I stayed fully clothed and continued kissing him. He tried to take my shirt off, but I wouldn't let him. Despite the fact that I was tiny at that age, I was insecure about my stomach. I always had been. So the shirt stayed, but I let him take off my pants. Before I could even catch my breath, he had two fingers inside of me. It didn't feel good, but I moaned quietly as if it did. He jammed those two, long fingers in and out a few times until finally I pushed him away.

I made up an excuse so I wouldn't seem lame or child-like.

"I can't today, I have to be home soon. I want to, though." I reasoned.

He tried to change my mind for a few minutes, but I was already dressed and basically out of the door. A text popped up on my pink razor cell phone when I was almost home,

"Wut u doin on Sat?" it read.

I let my mind race for a moment before I replied. Was I really ready? No, but was I going to do it, anyway? Absolutely. Like I said, I was willing to do anything to get this boy to like me.

"Nothing planned. Come over." I responded boldly.

For the rest of the week I spent my free time on google, searching things like "does your first time hurt?" or "do you bleed when you have sex for the first time?" Nervous didn't even begin to explain how I was feeling. I was scared, anxious, uncomfortable. But above all, I wanted to be wanted. If losing my virginity was the way to do it, I was prepared; or at least that's what I thought.

Saturday crept up on me quickly. My mom left the
house for work around noon, leaving me with the whole
place to myself. As soon as she walked out of the door, I
began my preparations. I started by cleaning up my
room. I took a long, hot shower, making sure to shave
every inch of my body, even my arms. I wanted to feel
soft and smell sweet. After my shower, I lathered up
some rose petal scented lotion. I put a dab on my lady
parts to ensure she was extra soft and sweet. (I didn't
know at that age scented lotion could cause yeast
infections. Oops.) I brushed my teeth, twice. I put on a
full face of make-up, and picked out an outfit that was
form-fitting but cozy. I wanted to look like I wasn't trying
too hard, even though I was. I chose black leggings and a
white tank-top. Underneath I wore the sexiest bra and
underwear I could find. Since I was basically a child, my
options were limited. It was a nude pair of lacy
underwear and a non-matching baby blue bra. Once I
was all clean and pretty, I texted Calen and told him he
could come over.

"Aight" was his response. I waited 30 minutes, which felt
like 30 hours, pacing back and forth in the house,
constantly checking my breath, and checking my face in
the mirror.

Finally, my doorbell rang. Calen was standing
there, but he wasn't alone. He brought a friend with him.
I was confused, didn't he know what I had planned?
Didn't he want privacy? I started to feel like some type of
sideshow. Like he needed a witness, so they could both

brag to the rest of their boys. This is what my gut told me. Unfortunately, I wasn't advanced in the arts of trusting my instincts at this point. So I wearily let them both in. We all sat together in my living room for a while. We had one of those big, suede, L-shaped couches. Calen and his friend sat on one end, I was at the other. It was awkward at first, but eventually Calen got up and sat next to me. He pulled me in closer, wrapping one arm around my neck. I laid my head on his chest, letting myself relax a bit. We stayed like this for a moment, until he stood up and tugged on my hand.

"Come on." he asserted. Somehow, without ever being in my house before, he lead me to my own room. His friend stayed, sitting on the couch, watching TV.

My room was fairly plain. I didn't have any posters, minimal pictures. There was a dresser, a desk, a mirror, and a futon instead of a bed. I already had the futon pulled out. Calen laid me down on it, without hesitation, as if this was a move he had practiced plenty of times. He kissed me for barely a moment before getting right down to business. I guess foreplay was the one thing he wasn't good at. He pulled my pants off, and attempted to shove a finger inside of me. I was completely dry, which we both felt. I thought this meant that *I* was doing something wrong. His solution was to lick his hand and then proceed. His finger went in a little easier this time, but it still didn't feel good by any means.

After the finger, quickly came the rest of him. Thankfully, he fell into me slowly. I stopped him about half way and told him that it hurt. He told me to relax, and continued. I tried so hard to do just that. I tried so hard to enjoy it, but I just couldn't. Nothing about it was pleasurable. It was painful and premature. It wasn't even slightly sexy or romantic. I let him continue for less than five minutes while I winced and eventually couldn't take it anymore. I pushed him off of me and yelled

"Okay!" I paused, "I'm sorry, I can't." As if I hadn't already.

"You serious?"

"It hurts." I said, half-way ashamed.

He seemed proud of himself, like that's what he was going for, like that meant he was so well-endowed, and not that I was a fourteen year old virgin with a fourteen year old vagina.

"Damn, alright. Ima go then."

"Oh. Okay." I hesitated, although I'm not sure what I expected.

I guess I wanted him to convince me to try again. I wanted him to talk me through it. I wanted him to understand that this was all new to me, and to be sweet about it. But Calen was not a sweet boy, that's particularly why I liked him.

And that was it. He walked out the front door, along with his friend. That's all he wanted. I knew it, immediately. I knew I probably wouldn't hear from him again. Suddenly I felt so dirty and wrong. It felt like parent teacher conference with Mrs.Gwell all over again. I sat on my big L-shaped couch and cried. With my knees tucked to my chest and my head buried between my knees, I cried.

I was more embarrassed than I was sad. I didn't feel sorry for myself, I just felt stupid. I felt like one of the silly girls my mother told me not to be. I wanted to cry for that girl, for the girl that I had become. So I did. I still do, sometimes.

Volume IV

Michael

For the sake of staying true to the timeline, let's talk about how messy the rest of my freshmen year of high school was. After losing my virginity to the worst person possible, I was a bit lost. I bounced around a lot between friends and phases. I hung out with so many different people and did so many different things. I was all over the place, but I enjoyed it. I enjoyed pretending to be someone I wasn't, because I wasn't happy with who I was.

Somewhere along the way I met Michael. I can't tell you exactly when or how we met, and I don't remember the moment I gained such an interest in him. But I will never forget our relationship; he was my first long-term boyfriend, and undoubtedly my first real love. Michael was a Junior, two years older than me, which meant he had a license and a cute little black maxima that I loved riding around with him in. He called it "Maxwell." Although Michael was flirtatious, he really wasn't the player type. He was just a goofball. His laugh was so contagious, I can still hear his voice in the back of my head saying "Maaaaan that's craaaazy" every time somebody would tease him for being the shortest kid on the basketball team.

Everyone loved him, but nobody loved him like I did. I fell for that boy fast and hard. Being with Michael was the first time that things felt light, fun and without so much pressure. I didn't have to act a certain way, I didn't have to do anything I didn't want to do. Although we weren't one of those sappy, heart-eyed couples, I knew he loved me. We had a good thing together, because we had a good time together.

We used to skip class to hang out at his house while his parents were gone. We would just lay up, watch TV, talk, and laugh. We would show up to all of the high school functions together, and I loved being seen with him. It wasn't a territorial feeling, it was a proud one. Sometimes we would just drive around together, smoke a blunt, and park somewhere quiet. Whatever we did, it was special. Our company was good, our conversation was good, our connection was good. I loved being with him.

Michael wasn't a virgin, and even though I wasn't either, I still felt like one at heart. My first experience was barely an experience, and I wasn't particularly eager to have another one. I never felt forced or pushed to move at a faster pace with Michael, but it did sit in the back of my mind. At times he would bring it up in a joking manner, saying something like

"Come on, Kira. When you gonna let me change your life? I'll give you my last name if I gotta."

 I would smile and brush it off. But I thought about it.
Sometimes I would worry that if he didn't get it from me,
he would get it from somebody else. About 4 months into
our relationship, I finally gave in. Sex with Michael
wasn't phenomenal or anything, but it wasn't bad, either.
At least this time it was for the right reasons. There were
genuine feelings involved. Honestly, I still had no idea
what I was doing. I didn't know how to communicate
during sex, I didn't even really understand what it was
supposed to feel like. It always hurt for the first few
minutes, and would slowly become more tolerable. It
was never something I jumped to do, but I didn't mind
doing it after I had gotten used to it. I definitely never
had an orgasm, although I got pretty good at pretending.
I remember thinking, everyone else must be faking it too,
there is no way any girl can enjoy this. But I loved
Michael, and he made me feel safe. He made me feel
wanted, and loved abundantly, not despite of but
because of my big-mixed-up-constantly-changing
personality. It felt like he loved the innermost workings
of me, and I still appreciate him for that. So yes, the sex
was mediocre, barely enjoyable, and mostly missionary,
but I wanted to make him happy. As a teenager, I didn't
understand that doing things you didn't necessarily
enjoy to make a boy happy could potentially be
detrimental to your sense of self in the long run.
Actually, I'm still figuring that out. Anyways, let's stay on

topic. I was in love, and everything I was doing for
Michael was because of that love.

Don't get me wrong, we had our problems. There
were times when we would fight, a lot. There were
always rumors, and I was quick to believe them. I
accused him of cheating on me several times, although I
don't think he ever actually did. Just the thought of it
made my blood boil. Soon, I hated any girl he came into
contact with. I became jealous, and possessive. Honestly,
I think he liked the possessive part a bit, and it's not like
he didn't reciprocate that. Everybody knew that I was
with Michael, everyone knew not to try it with me. But
still, we fought. We fought when he would ditch me for
his friends, we fought when my smart mouth got the best
of me, we fought when we ran into his exes, we fought
when I interrogated him. And when we fought, it was
frivolous. We acted like children, saying things we didn't
mean, blocking each others numbers, slamming doors
and driving off. We both had the habit of making a scene
in order to prove a point.

Just as I don't remember exactly when I gained
interest in Michael, I don't remember exactly when or
why we broke up. It was very much back and forth for
quite a while, so eventually it all became a blur. I do
remember breaking up more than once. Throughout our
two years of being involved together, we went on roughly
five or six breaks. Some lasted no more than a few days
and some lasted months, in which we would see other
people in the meantime. Neither of us got as serious with

anybody else as we were with each other, so we always just sort of naturally ended up right where we started. I remember it always felt so casual, like we had never broken up in the first place.

I think eventually we just grew apart. We both got older, and we learned things about ourselves. Honestly, many of the things I learned about myself thanks to him. As I mentioned, he was a Junior when I first met him. Soon he was graduated and leaving the state for school. At that point we were already halfway done with the relationship, so the distance finished the job for us. I don't remember ever being angry with him, or hating him in the slightest. I remember making sarcastic remarks towards each other when one of us found out the other was dating someone new. But just like always, it was out of love.

In fact, Michael and I stayed in touch for a while after we ended things for good. He checked up on me often, whether it was just sending a text or setting a skype date. We would reminisce about the past and discuss the present. Sometimes we would even touch on the possibility of the future, specifically the possibility of a future together. I don't think either of us were ever completely serious, but I think we could have been.

With each year, we talked less. Sometimes we would go months, sometimes a whole year without speaking to each other. I never took it personally, we were both busy leading different lives. I think I changed

a lot more than he did. It felt like every time we did get
the chance to talk, I was a part of a whole new world
while his current events stayed mostly the same. It's
been over two years now. The last time we spoke he was
in a relationship, and messaged me saying that he
wanted me to talk to his girlfriend for him. I was a little
confused because even before then it had been a while
since we spoke last, I couldn't possibly guess what it
could be about. He explained that somehow she was
under the impression that he was cheating on her with
me. I still don't understand how that happened, but I did
him the favor and messaged her explaining that it was
false. He thanked me, and we continued to chat for a bit,
but with the situation at hand we figured it probably
wasn't a good idea to carry on for too long.

I still wonder about him from time to time. I
caught myself searching through our old pictures on
Facebook the other day. I am still grateful for the times
that we had, and the relationship that we built. It was
never a dull moment, and looking back I know that I was
truly loved by him. I think about the pieces of me that
have stemmed from him. He instilled a sense of lightness
in me. One of my most desired traits in a lover today, is
someone who I can be casual and comfortable around.
He showed me the importance and the beauty in that. I
would tell him that if I could, but I don't even think I
have his number anymore. Maybe I'll try someday.
Maybe he will.

Volume V

James

Most of my "in-between time lovers" are not worth mentioning. Compared to Michael, almost all of them were meaningless and short lived. I couldn't even tell you all of their names if I wanted to; that information wasn't important enough for my brain to keep stored. There was, however, one relevant experience I had with a not-so-relevant boy.

I used to throw a lot of parties, the duplex I lived in that year was almost made for it. The upstairs was off-limits, with my mom and little brother's room being up there. The main floor was treated as a sort of laid-back spot. People would hang out in the living room and kitchen, either chatting or playing drinking games. The basement, which was actually my room, was treated as a dance floor. People really went at it down there. They would turn the lights off, blast slow-grind music, and rub themselves all over one another. One night, when everyone left and the lights came back on, I found two condoms on my floor. My mom had just started dating the man who is now her husband, and she spent a lot of time at his house. At this point in my life, my mom and I were fairly close. She trusted me and gave me the freedom to make my own decisions and learn from my own mistakes. So all in all, I had the perfect situation to throw iconic parties, and I did.

Everyone who was anyone came, and we all got along and had a great time. James and his group of friends were usually present at my parties. James was two years older than me. He was tall, with a halfway grown in beard and braces. His braces sometimes made it sound like his mouth was full of spit. Looking back, I'm not entirely sure what drew me to him. I mean sure, he was popular, he was sort of funny, definitely entertaining. Other than that, I'm not sure. I never really learned too much about him. I remember hearing that his parents were either dead or in another state and he lived with his uncle, but we never really talked about things like that. We never really talked about much at all, at least not in great detail.

When I first met James, he was interested in my best friend. My best friend had absolutely no interest in him. She led him on for a bit, until eventually deciding to break the news to him. He was constantly asking me,

"What's up with Chelsey? Is she feeling me? You gonna put a good word in for me?"

To which I would respond, "Yeah, yeah. Of course, I will."

For a while, James and I were friends. I loved hanging out with him, and we referred to each other as "bro" and "sis." Ironically, our nature was a bit flirtatious, but we brushed it off as part of our personalities. Whenever people would ask us if we were a "thing," aka hooking up, we would laugh and deny it as if that would never happen because we just didn't see each other that way.

One night, at one of my infamous parties, things took a bit of a turn. James and his boys were there, but my best friend wasn't, she was out of town. Everyone was drinking and feeling good, I was hanging out in the kitchen with James and a few of his other friends. I remember James eating mac and cheese, and I remember dancing around the kitchen providing all of my guests with mediocre entertainment. And the next thing I remember; James was laughing, and he looked at me and said,

"Come here and give me a kiss." and I didn't even think about it.

I followed those orders, exactly. I remember he tasted like the mac and cheese that he hadn't even finished swallowing when I kissed him. But we were drunk, and we didn't care. Somehow a kiss turned into confessions of our feelings for each other and the next day I woke up and knew I had some explaining to do.

Even though my best friend had decided she wasn't interested in James, I still felt icky for what I did. After all, however brief it may have been, they did spend a romantic moment together. It was too late for girl code, I had already determined that I wanted to be with James. One woman's trash is another woman's treasure, I thought. I was just hoping that Chelsey would understand and give me her blessing. James and I had been talking on the phone, discussing how we would break the news. I would admit to her what happened the night previously, and explain that in the moment it was stupid and meaningless. We were just drunk and messing around. Then I would explain that after sobering up, we had talked about it and realized we liked each other and if, and only if she was okay with it, we would start seeing each other. Chelsey had been my best friend for a couple of years, and she was already into a different guy, so I genuinely thought she wouldn't care.

Things didn't go over so smoothly. I texted Chelsey as soon as I hung up with James. I laid it all out in one long message. It took her three hours to respond, and I was sweating at the anticipation. I wasn't, and I'm still not a confrontational person. Situations like these stress me out more than they should because I don't like to upset people. I am a people pleaser. When Chelsey finally got back to me, she didn't seem happy, but I couldn't exactly tell her tone through text. She responded with something along the lines of

"K. Can we talk when I get back? Idk how I feel about this."

"Oh. Sure, of course." I replied.

She got back later that night, and drove over to my house.

The conversation didn't last long, it was clear that we were on different pages. Chelsey expressed that if I was a good friend, I wouldn't even put her in this position. She said she wasn't comfortable with it, and couldn't believe I thought she would be. I expressed that if she was a good friend, she would want me to be happy. I called her selfish, and a few other names. I don't know what came over me, but my attitude switched completely. I was no longer tip-toeing around my friend's feelings. I was going to get what I wanted, one way or another. She wasn't going to stand in my way. I put the final nail in the coffin with

"You are just thirsty for attention. You can't stand for anyone else to have it. You're jealous. It's pathetic."

And that was it. Our friendship was exterminated. The other couple of friends that I had took Chelsey's side, and so all I had was my temporary lover. For the next few months I spent most of my time with him. I had a few other friends, and I was on the cheer team, so I kept busy. But still, I knew that something was missing. A sense of regret sat in my chest for a while before I ever acknowledged it.

James and I were okay together. It definitely wasn't what I thought it would be, but we were okay. We mostly hung out at his house, or mine. We didn't go in public much. Really, the only positive thing that came out of that scenario was the most amazing oral sex I've ever had. Even with those braces of his, he knew what he was doing. One day, after going down on me for an hour, I went upstairs to go to the bathroom only to notice that my clit was completely enlarged. It was the first time I had ever seen it like that. It was sensitive to the touch.

All sexual experiences aside, I never completely shook the guilt of being with James. I had managed to convince myself that I was right for awhile. I had managed to assure myself and all of my new friends that I was the victim. I sold the story that I was thankful to shake off such toxic friends. But if all of this was true, why did I still feel so weird about it?

Eventually James went back to his long-term, on-and-off girlfriend that, for some reason, I believed he was really through with this time. I made my way back to Michael for a little while. He wasn't incredibly happy with me either, being that him and James were friends.

In retrospect, I became somebody I didn't really like for someone that barely liked me. I could no longer blame other people for being upset with me. I lost my closest friends because I was being selfish, and a little desperate. These things became apparent to me, and I eventually reached out to apologize.

Chelsey and my other friends happily accepted my apology and offered one back. I hardly deserved it, and was a little surprised, but I was eager to put the whole thing behind us.

Really, the only reason James is worth mentioning is because of the lesson that came with him. I realized the importance of female friendship, and just how temporary lovers can be. My focus shifted a bit. While I was still infatuated with the idea of love and being in love, I felt less compelled to fall completely obsessed with every boy I became romantic with. I started to understand what it meant to be a woman, and how to be good to other women. We catch enough slack from the rest of the world, it is necessary to show respect for each other. This was a mistake I never made again, one I would never even think of. I became an honorary follower of the girl code, and it didn't stop me from finding love once. Lesson of the day: he's probably not worth it. Don't go there.

Volumes VI-VIII

Riley, Pete, and Rick

By my senior year of high school, I was the epitome of young, wild, and free with the same hunger for male attention, (thanks, dad) and the habit of getting bored easily. I never really had an intentional type, but at some point, I realized I hadn't dated any of the giant array of preppy white boys at my school. I couldn't even recall ever being approached by one, and suddenly, I was intrigued. My high school lover was no longer in high school, and I was up for a challenge. I figured, why not try something new? I'd like to point out just how out of character this is for me. Usually, I go out of my way to avoid men like my father. Something about the way they abuse every ounce of privilege they have, or their sense of entitlement, or their consistent racist and sexist comments, or maybe it's just their extremely short-shorts with boat patterns that throw me off. Anyways, I was watching a lot of *Gossip Girl* at the time and felt the need to test the Chuck Bass territory.

I wasn't exactly the type of girl you would assume that type of guy would date. I was a little rough around the edges. I didn't necessarily enjoy country music, or shopping at Ralph Lauren and J-Crew. And of course, there was that pesky reputation of mine, the high school slut. Preppy white boys typically go for preppy white girls, girls who carry themselves with purity and class, girls who cross their legs and plan their weddings. That just wasn't me.

Despite all of these things I knew to be true, I made an effort anyways (I still blame *Gossip Girl*). I figured, they couldn't all be terrible (spoiler alert, I was wrong). I wouldn't know unless I tried. So, I began purposely expressing interest in guys that I wouldn't normally go for. For the most part, and to my own surprise, there wasn't a guy that I struggled to seduce. I began to understand the power of sexuality, and just how easy men can be. But still, with that crowd, it always felt like I had something to prove. I always felt the need to tweak my personality a bit in order to fit in or avoid judgement.

So, I did a little tweaking and then I met Riley. Riley was incredibly tall, he played baseball, and his father was a judge. He was a little goofy looking in the face, but attractive enough. He fell head over heels for me, and fast. I let him finger me a couple of times and made several excuses not to sleep with him. After about two months, I cut things off. I just wasn't feeling things with him, and I'm not sure how else to explain that.

Then came Pete. I was actually very much into Pete. He was handsome, smart, funny, and probably the first boy in pastel colors that I was sexually drawn to. Our entire relationship was based on sex, really. He liked the fact that I was a little different than his previous girlfriend. He never said it, but I could tell. Pete took me to prom, and we had a cute little run full of lunch-break sex and late-night car sex. I think we had sex everywhere except for each other's houses. Unfortunately, our sweet run ended when I got a batch of sour news. After going to Planned Parenthood to refill my birth control, and receiving my mandatory STI exam, I was told I had chlamydia. I was horrified. I had no idea where it came from. I was young and didn't understand what I know now about STI's, including how common chlamydia is. I was humiliated, and so scared to tell Pete. I wasn't sure if I had given it to him, because we used condoms, but I still felt it would be wrong to hide it. I was hoping he would be understanding and make me feel better about the whole situation when I called him in tears. Pete assured me that it was alright. He asked me to get the medication for him, and he would pick it up from me. After he got his medication, he blocked me completely and never spoke to me again.

Then there was Rick. Rick was one of the more laid back preps I dated. Talking to him was definitely easier, I was able to behave more like myself. He was a shorter guy with a baby face and the cutest little mole above his lip. I wanted to pinch his cheeks more than I wanted to sleep with him. I assume he was used to this reaction, because he definitely had a tendency to overcompensate. Yes, Rick had a severe case of small man syndrome. His Instagram was full of pictures of him

with beautiful girls; an obvious effort to prove
something. If you look at it now, you will see that
nothing has changed. One new years eve, Rick and I
attended a house party together and got drunk enough to
lock ourselves in a room and make out for hours. He was
trying to have sex with me, and I was going to let him,
but the whiskey got the best of his abilities. He couldn't
get it up, and I was ready to give up when he looked at
me and said

"Would it be okay if I told my friends we did it,
anyways?"

To be completely honest, I felt bad for the kid. It was
clear he wasn't the most experienced guy in the game,
and he definitely had some insecurity issues going on. I
looked at him sideways with a little disbelief, but mostly
pity, and I agreed.

"Sure, why not? We were going to, anyways."

He didn't hesitate to tell every single one of his friends
and acquaintances that he had gotten into my pants. He
must have told the story with real conviction, because
people were asking me about it for weeks.

I broke things off with Rick shortly after. He got
what he wanted, a boost in his reputation and some

credit from his boys. I got what I needed, a dose of reality. I was searching for approval in boys like my father when I was reminded that the male ego, specifically the ego of a conservative, wealthy, white, preppy, adolescent boy is one of the most fragile things in the world. It is so dangerously fragile, that when threatened, they will go to great lengths to preserve it. These lengths can be much more terrifying than a block on Facebook or a fabricated story, but that is something I will bring up later.

Volume IX

Z

This next volume is going to come off as rather out of place, and it is. I contemplated the best time to bring him up in this brief saga, and really no place feels perfect. I thought it best to keep him in order with the timeline, if no place else. Z deserves a place in this collection of stories, to be acknowledged and immortalized as a momentary lover and beautiful friend.

I met Z during my senior year of high school through mutual friends. He had a large supply of people who loved him, solely due to his personality. His personality was one that could never be mimicked and could certainly never be forgotten. He was full of laughter, and whoever was in his presence felt completely at ease and supported. Z didn't become "conventionally attractive" until a year or so after graduation, but he had a way to him that drew me in immediately. We became friends quickly. We would hang out almost every day after school, and we were inseparable on the weekends.

I think Z and I were so connected because we were one in the same. We were slightly different than the rest of our friend group, not quite outcasts, but definitely distanced. Neither of us were extremely revealing about our inner selves. We weren't necessarily revealing with one another either, but I think we had a sort of unspoken understanding. Our friendship was the type that you could comfortably sit there in silence for hours, just soaking in the joy of each others presence. I loved doing things with Z, it always felt easy.

About a month into our blossoming friendship, Z and I had become a little closer than I had expected. Eventually the topic of potentially being a couple was brought up. We approached the topic as an issue of common sense. We already spent all of our time together, and we were at least semi attracted to each other, and we were both currently a little lonely. So, we decided to give it a shot. It seemed like the logical thing to do. We let our friends know about our decision the next day, and while mine were momentarily shocked, but ultimately happy for us, most of his friends were kind of dicks about it. They insisted it was fake and turned it into a joke. I'm assuming it's because every last one of them had attempted to have sex with me at one point, and Z was the last person they assumed I'd give it up to.

Truthfully, nothing changed much. Z and I continued behaving the way we always did. We didn't dive straight into PDA, or any version of affection really. We kissed sometimes, and laid together hand in hand, but our sexual intimacy was pretty much nonexistent. It's not that I wasn't interested, and I knew he wanted to try, but something in me wasn't ready to cross over to that side just yet.

Skipping ahead a few months, (another spoiler alert) Z and I did end up having sex one night. Ironically, it was after we had broken up. It was after the Vice Versa dance, I had rented a cheap hotel room for a few friends and I to drink and hang out. He ended up staying the night with me, and we finally had our moment. It was brief, and a little awkward, but it felt like something long overdue.

Now, back to the story at hand. Nothing Z and I did felt very romantic. However, being that I have an addictive personality, I got very caught up in the idea of us. I lost track of the friendship for a moment, and started trying to build an intense relationship that just wasn't a reality. We loved each other, we cared for one another, but we weren't in love. I became confused, and he noticed. After a couple of months, Z broke things off with me.

I was laying in my bed when I received the call.

"Kira, we need to talk. Hear me out, please don't take it personally. I think I want to be single, again. If we're being honest with each other, we both know we should be friends. If you want to be. Can we be? I'm sorry."

I did take it personally. I was crushed. My best friend dumped me, and my ego didn't take it lightly. No, I didn't want to be friends. I was scorned. For a moment, at least.

This rage didn't last long. I came to my senses a little over a week later. Z had given me my space, and allowed me to be upset. I was thankful for that. I knew I didn't want to let go of him completely. He was, after all, my best friend. He was there for me, always. If I ever needed anything, if I ever called crying, he was there to pick me up within ten minutes. He was good to me. I didn't want to let go of that.

I texted him and apologized for reacting the way I did. I told him that I did still want to be friends, and I understood his decision. He explained that there was no one else, he just saw things heading in a direction he didn't want to go. I agreed.

Unfortunately, things weren't the same after our attempt at romantic love. That's usually how it goes though, isn't it? We remained friends, but we certainly were not as close as before. We never drifted completely apart, we always kept in contact. We stayed in the same inner circles, so we ran into each other often. But I never quite got over the loss of the genuine friendship that we had built. Z had a sweet soul, he meant no harm for any human. Being in his life was an uplifting experience, one that I mourned the loss of.

Z committed suicide in 2016. He texted me the night before. He asked me for a ride home, but I didn't have a car, so I offered to call him an Uber instead. What I didn't know was that it wasn't just a ride he needed, it was someone to talk to. It was Z's cry for help, and I missed it. I still have not fully forgiven myself for failing him that night. I will never shake the feeling that there was something I could have done. But we all make decisions in life. Z and I made the decision to force a relationship which resulted in the downfall of a perfectly platonic friendship. Three years later Z made the decision to end his life. He left no note, no explanation, no goodbye. He left nothing but his memory. Now not only me, but the handfuls of people who loved him dearly are doing their best to be thankful for the opportunity they had to participate in his life. We miss you, we forgive you, we love you Z.

Volume X

Justin

As I moved on and into adulthood, I slowly began to understand who I was as a lover. My concept of love was less juvenile than before, and I was thinking more about my future and who would be a part of it. My relationships, and the feelings attached to them became much more intense. You will notice, the remaining volumes will be a bit more mature, as the timeline shifts into my college and post-college years. However, this next lover of mine is an incredibly complicated one. Similar to the previous volume, no place seemed completely appropriate to start. There is no way to "fit him in" because the amount of space and time he took up was monumental. In order to get the full experience, I have to take you back to my elementary days. Yes, this man has been around for most of my life. Of course, back then I had no idea he would be such a building block in my ideas of love and end up causing me a disgusting amount of chaos, but here we are.

Justin and I had grown up together. We had seen each other grow from scrawny-armed-buck-toothed children, and into our adult bodies. We had shared playgrounds, shared classes, and shared friends. Justin and I became closer acquaintances in middle school, having regular conversations in the one class we had together and occasionally in the hallway. We became closer friends in the beginning years of high school. It was a slow blooming friendship, but eventually, at one point, we were doing everything together. My family ended up moving into a duplex that was less than two blocks from his house, leaving plenty of opportunity for us to spend time together.

It was casual at first. We joked around and talked about things that didn't really matter. Justin was always quite the comedian and was never afraid to laugh at himself. He was also very smart though, his family did a brilliant job at preparing him for a successful life. He was the type of person that could get along with anybody. He was the type of person that everyone knew would be good at anything he wanted to do. I was always a little jealous of him. I'm not sure at what point things shifted into something more than casual. When I ask him how he remembers it, he claims that I turned him down quite a few times before I let him in. Apparently, there was a moment that he went in for a kiss and I blatantly denied him. I don't remember it this way, but I suppose there are two sides to every story. Maybe the truth is somewhere in the middle.

I recall it as a gradual shift, similar to the rest of our relationship. The more time we spent together, the more interested I became. One day, we went to the gym together, and I chatted while he lifted weights. He was in football and basketball, so working out was part of his daily regimen. I remember him asking me for relationship advice, which threw me off a bit. I always pictured Justin as the kind of guy who would stay a virgin until college and stay semi-awkward for the rest of his life. Something about knowing that other girls might have been interested in him made me look at him in a different light. Maybe I always had those feelings for him and didn't want to admit it, or maybe my motives were purely shallow. Whatever the reason, this shift changed everything.

The next day, Justin and I went for a walk by the lake in our neighborhood. The weather was gorgeous, and the mood felt new. It felt like we both had realized our feelings for one another, it was just a matter of saying it out loud. I went first. I let it all out. I told him that I liked him as more than a friend, and that I wasn't suggesting a full-fledged relationship but that if he felt the same, we should give each other a fair chance romantically. Of course, sixteen year old me probably didn't let the news out so eloquently. It probably came out more as a run-on sentence without punctuation, but I think I got my point across. He kissed me. And in that moment, I knew what I wanted. I knew it was him. I knew people wouldn't approve because we didn't make any sense as a couple. I knew that his superficial friends would have opinions about my promiscuous reputation and his family would be concerned about me corrupting his innocence. I knew that things wouldn't fall into place so easily, but I knew I wanted him anyway. This mentality has really put me through the ringer. Here I am, seven years later, still juggling and coping with the damage it has done. But let's not get ahead of ourselves.

Justin and I had a couple of good months. We saw movies, we ate ice cream, we went on walks, on drives, snuck into each others homes when the hours got too late. We kissed a lot, he slowly got better at it. Our time together was full of foreplay, but he wasn't exactly boneable material yet. He still had a sense of innocence, and I wasn't sure how I felt about taking his virginity. I was nervous, because although I was no virgin, I wasn't exactly a pro. I usually slept with guys more experienced than myself, so I wouldn't have to worry. Things were different with Justin. I was always a little scared of embarrassing myself in front of him. I always wanted to look my best, speak my best, be my best with him. His opinion mattered to me.

It didn't take long for things to get messy. The girl that Justin had previously asked for my advice on, Sydney, became his girlfriend. He told me that she had called him, saying that she still wanted to be with him, but that he had plans to turn her down. When that didn't happen, his excuse was that she had been crying and that he felt terrible and didn't want to hurt her. I guess he had no problem hurting me, I was damaged goods already, right? I was furious, and heartbroken. Just as I started feeling comfortable with him, trusting him, envisioning a real relationship with him, we were done.

It was the first of many heartbreaks provided by my dear old Justin.

Justin and I stayed in contact through his relationship with Sydney. Not too many people knew about our attempted amorous relationship, so we were able to continue as halfway friends. I didn't see much of him, though, until, things got even messier.

I start hearing and seeing more of Justin. He starts telling me that he misses me, and he should have never left me for Sydney. He starts telling me everything I want to hear, and it doesn't take long for it to go to my head. He kisses me, I kiss him back, and now he is a cheater and I am a homewrecker. But we don't care. We don't care what people think, we don't care who is getting hurt. We are selfish and we are full of desire and we do what we want to each other, and to everybody else. This is the foundation of our situationship.

Eventually, Sydney finds out what's going on. Justin gets dumped and another tally is added to my reputation. It doesn't bother me much, I am just happy to have Justin back to myself. I am under the belief that things will go back to the way they once were, and we will pick up right where we left off. It feels like this for a moment, but when I start insinuating that we be together officially, Justin doesn't seem too excited about the idea. He claims that he wants to, but follows up with a handful of excuses on why he can't or we shouldn't. I'm not sure why he is less interested in the idea this time around, and I start to feel like I've done something wrong. I start to feel like there is something about me that isn't good enough. I grew up knowing that if a boy wants to be with you, nothing will stop him. So I knew something was wrong, but I went along with it anyway. I let myself believe everything he said. I allowed myself to make excuses for him.

Soon enough, he was in a new relationship, and it wasn't with me. It was a new girl, similar to Sydney. Much more quiet, much more subtle, much more conventionally appropriate for Justin than I was. Once again, I am hurt. Even more so this time around, because his new relationship only solidifies my belief that there is something wrong with me. I start to feel like his dirty little secret. Once again, he finds his way back to me. Once again, I give in. Once again, he is a cheater, I am a homewrecker. And this becomes our pattern.

Eventually, I stopped waiting around. I started seeing other people too. But of course, this didn't change much. Justin and I spent years in and out of relationships with other people, and in and out of a situationship with one another. We became chronic cheaters. Every relationship we got into would end because we couldn't stay away from each other. We were consistently inconsistent. Maybe he liked the chase, maybe I just wanted something I couldn't have. Whatever the reason, we had a hold on each other. The older we got, the less innocent Justin was. After our first time having sex in the Summer of 2013, we could no longer be just friends. I was undeniably attracted to him. Our sexual chemistry was off the charts. Whenever we were around each other, something was bound to happen.

I think that subconsciously, we did it all on purpose. I must have been some sort of masochist, because I was addicted to the emotional pain that he caused me. I began to egg it on, like I wanted it to happen. If I knew that he was seeing someone else, I would go out of my way to run into him. I would make sure I was looking my best, and I would give him this look that meant that I wanted him. It was a look he could never refuse. He started to refer to me as his kryptonite, and I loved it. I secretly loved the back and forth, the endless run-around. I know he did, too. It was toxic, and detrimental to my sense of self. It skewed my idea of what love is, and made it close to impossible for me to be in a real relationship. But did any of that stop me? Of course not. And if I'm being totally real with myself, that issue didn't start with him.

In hindsight, I understand more so why I was so attached to this type of relationship. I think it mimicked the very relationship I had with my father. My father was my first lesson in love. He showed me what it means to be loved by a man. He lead by example, leaving me with the impression that unavailable and difficult is real love. He ingrained in me the idea that love is meant to be hard, it's meant to hurt. Just as my father went months, sometimes years without reaching out to me, Justin had

the same habit. Just as he could never truly give me the
relationship I needed and deserved, I started to realize
Justin wouldn't either.

Nevertheless, I continued to try. It took me years
to come to this realization, and by then, I was already
completely devoted. So we continued with the back and
forth throughout college. We would get into bed with
each other every time we were both visiting home. I even
went out of my way to take a train to him a few times.
Eventually, I was sort of comfortable with it. Our
situationship grew on me. Sure, I wasn't getting
everything I wanted, but at least I knew we would always
be a part of each others lives. We managed to creep up
on each other and latch in for good, and strangely, this
brought me comfort.

Justin continued to stay mostly emotionally
unavailable, and at some point I adapted to that. At some
point, I stopped believing that he would someday wake
up and realize what he was missing. I stopped expecting
something more. And of course, as soon as my attitude
changed, something ironic happened. It was like the
minute I started seeing things his way, the minute I
stopped blaming him for everything, the minute I
stopped trying to make him want more, he did. Suddenly
he got better at having meaningful conversations. He
started acknowledging his past faults, and apologizing
for taking so long to come around. He started making an
effort to build a real relationship. It felt like an overdue

miracle. He was offering everything I ever asked for on a silver platter. But this time, it wasn't enough for me.

I think I was so jaded by the previous five-six years, I was so emotionally drained, that I couldn't allow myself to give in. I couldn't trust Justin, and I was scared. I was scared that the moment I slipped up and began yearning as I once did, he would switch up on me again. So, here I was, in this strange state of limbo. On one hand, I knew that I could never let the history I have with this person go. I knew that I had put so much time and energy into this, and was still curious to see if it could work for real. On the other hand, I was hesitant and almost unable to release myself completely. Here was this man, that I have wanted for so long, that I have shown undeniable love towards no matter what. A man that knew me better than any other, who watched me grow, who was not afraid to call me out, who could make me laugh until it hurt. A man that I had shared an unbreakable connection with, who I have shared long-lasting memories with. A man who played such a role in my life, I knew he would never just disappear. Here he was, standing before me, offering me everything. But I couldn't take it.

For a while, I was angry at him. I blamed him for my inability to get close. I told him that he was the reason I am the way I am. He was apologetic and willing to give me my space. But of course, him talking about space just came off to me as a way to get rid of me, once again. Everything just felt painfully familiar, and I couldn't shake that. So for the first time, I walked away.

Justin and I didn't speak for a year after that. I thought about him often, and in an effort to avoid repeating old habits I blocked him on every form of social media. However, I never blocked his number. I couldn't get myself to do it, despite everyone telling me that it needed to be done. The way I saw it, was I had experienced the loss of people close to me before. I have experienced the feeling of missing that final chance to say goodbye. That wound was still fresh. I didn't necessarily think something like this would happen, but I knew that I would care if it did. I knew that I would care if something bad happened to Justin, and I felt obligated to be available if he ever needed me.

Nothing came up, and the silence continued. I thought a lot about our final conversation, and I began questioning whether or not I spoke the truth or just my version of it. Obviously Justin wasn't innocent, but did I play a part in our failure? I went back and forth in my head often, but I continued on with my life anyways. I started a new life in Chicago. I got a new job, a new apartment, new roommates, and a new boyfriend. (No worries, his chapter is coming up soon enough.) I was content with where I was in the world, I felt like a better version of myself than I was the year before. Things were good, and I was happy.

My birthday was rolling around the corner, and I
was sort of curious to see if I would hear from Justin. I
always get an intuition about these things, almost as if I
can will them to happen. And just like clockwork, he
texted me at 11:59 pm, a minute before my birthday was
over.

"Happy Birthday! Have a good one kid, you deserve it. I
hope this year has been alright for you."

 My stomach turned a bit, like it always does. I didn't
know if I should respond, I didn't know what I would
say. I didn't want to fall back into the same routines, but
I didn't see any harm in a "thank you."

I slept on it. The next morning, I decided to
respond

"Thanks. Life has been good, I wish you the same."

Nothing flirtatious, nothing too inviting. Just enough to
say, *I appreciate you reaching out. No, I don't hate you.*
I thought that would be the end of it, and I was fine with
that. Like I said before, I was in a new relationship, and
this time it felt real and it felt satisfying. I didn't need to
chase after Justin anymore, I found somebody that filled
up every part of me. I also didn't want to upset my
boyfriend, he had an idea about my history with Justin

and I knew he wouldn't be too pleased if he saw his name pop up on my phone.

Later that day, I received another text.

"That's good to hear. Things decent over here. Anything new?"

Without thinking, I responded. It was like a natural reaction. Like nothing had changed.

"Nothing really. Same old. Just saving money and practicing my writing. What about you?"

As soon as I hit send, I regretted it. What was I doing? Why was I even bothering? What good could possibly come from this conversation? He would just tell me everything he knew I loved to hear and conflict me, causing problems in my new relationship. He was a professional at planting a seed in my mind that would never grow, but instead fester until I ruined whatever else I had going on.

"Man nothing really. I just been thinking a lot, lately." Here it was. I didn't want to respond, but I did.

"About what?" I was provoking it.

"Just everything you said last time we talked."

"What about it?"

"You really think all that about me? I mean damn, I know I needed to grow up and I feel bad that I put you through all that but you can't think it was all on me."

I was furious. Was he really trying to blame me? Was he really trying to deflect the responsibility? Before I could respond with an angry novel, my phone dinged again.

"I ain't tryna blame you. I just want a chance to explain myself. You always out here tryna turn me into the bad guy. I apologized for the past. I let other people, my friends get in the way of how I felt. I was scared to be with you. But you always acted funny with me, too. You would say you wanted to be with me but when I would try to show you any affection you ain't want it. You always put on this act and I couldn't get close to you forreal. Look, you always been there for me and shown me love no matter what. I appreciate the things you did for me. I wanted to be with you, I still do, but I know you

got you someone you love now. You in love forreal, I
respect that. I just wanted to clear the air."

These words, although through the screen of my
phone, were like the sweetest release, and the greatest
sense of closure I have ever felt. I never thought closure
was going to happen for Justin and I, I always thought it
would remain a giant question mark. I felt a sense of
forgiveness wash over me. And as it turns out,
forgiveness was the answer.

"Thank you for that," I responded, "I agree with you. It
wasn't all you. Please don't forget, you hurt me in a way
that nobody else has, but I also am responsible for why
we never really worked out. I know that although I talked
a big game, I was emotionally unavailable as well. I know
that I fed into all of the drama. I want you to know that
you will always have a friend in me. You will always have
a space in my heart. Thank you for teaching me many
things."

It was a ten minute conversation via text, but it
was exactly what I needed. I have known Justin for
years, so I knew just how hard it was for that man to say
those things. I knew he was probably racking his brain
for months about if and how he would say it. Because he
operated just like I did. I felt like my conflictions turned
into acceptance for what really was, and what is now.

Justin wasn't a bad person. He was a kid, who had
feelings that he didn't understand. He was immature,
and he didn't realize the ramifications of his actions. It's
unfortunate that I hoped for more from him than he
could give me, and that I allowed myself to build this
idea up in my head no matter how many times it was
crushed. But the everlasting situationship taught me so
much about myself; my weaknesses, and the strength of
my love. I know that both of us have grown because of it.
We were not made to be with one another, we were made
to help each other grow. We were meant to test one
another's ideas of themselves, and expand our capacity
to understand and forgive. I was happy that somebody I
have known all of my life, and who truly understands me
could remain a friend. I never thought such a thing was
possible.

I read somewhere that you will have the love of
your life, and the love for your life. The love of your life
will be hard, messy, and hurtful, but it will teach you
everything you need to know. The love for your life will
be the one to heal you, the one to take in all of your
baggage and love it unconditionally. I think I've found
that now.

No, I am not trying to make excuses for Justin.
No, we don't talk every day. No, we don't meet each
other out for coffee or drinks. It is not that type of
friendship. Actually, I haven't talked to him in months.
Every once in a while, there is a message on my phone,

"How is everything?" And a brief conversation follows. It is a quick check-in, and a quick reminder that yes, I am still here and yes, I do still care. We do not have to be in a back and forth, messy, obscure version of romantic relationship to honor our history. We respect each other for who we have grown into, and where we end up. Despite of, and because of all of this, I love him. But he is not the love *for* my life. And that's okay.

Volume XI

Jaden

While we're on the topic of long-term, but wishy-washy lovers, Jaden fits right in. For a long time, Jaden was a dear friend to me. We met through mutual friends early in our high school years. He wasn't afraid to crack jokes, and he quickly admitted that he was attracted to me. I was intrigued, I'll admit. I found Jaden cute. He was short, skinny, and a little awkward. I'm a sucker for those. He wasn't vain in the slightest. He was sweet, and easy to talk to. We didn't have much in common and still it was like we could talk the whole day away.

Jaden was not the most experienced with girls. He wasn't a virgin, but he may as well have been. While we could text all day about basically anything, he was very shy in person. He joked about how intimidating I was to him. I would literally have to beg him for weeks to hang out with me for two hours. And we couldn't be alone, he would only agree to meet up with me if there were friends there, a group. Of all my years knowing Jaden, I only hung out with him once. Me, him, my best friend Shayna, and his two best friends. We all sat in his basement and watched a movie. He sat on the other side of the room, on a twin bed, while the rest of us sat on the couch. I broke the ice, of course, by walking over to the bed to sit with him. He welcomed me, and even put his arm around me. I was proud. We didn't kiss, we barely touched, it was very PG.

After our mediocre cuddle session, the flirting started to escalate a bit. He would text me cute things every day, and we would go back and forth, teasing each other and talking about our day. After a while, Jaden admitted his feelings for me. It wasn't something I didn't already know, but it was a little difficult for me to take it seriously considering the fact that it was close to impossible to get him to spend time with me. So, I acknowledged his feelings, and I admitted that I could see myself being with him if he could actually make a real life effort. Of course, this never really happened, so I continued to have other relationships while maintaining my virtual one.

Every time I got a new boyfriend, or girlfriend, Jaden would get upset. He would send me a half angry, half hurt text. To which I would respond,

"I understand, and I'm sorry for hurting you. But, what do you expect? Am I supposed to wait around for you to grow the balls to hang out with me? I'm young, I'm going to live my life."

We would go a couple of weeks, maybe a month without speaking. Then, before I knew it, there would be a message from him. I'll admit, in the beginning I was a little cruel. I would still lead him on while I was in other relationships. To me it was harmless, Jaden and I were friends. Friends with flirty messages, at the most. But how could we be anything else without real interaction. And texting couldn't be considered cheating, could it?

Well, the older we got, the more intense our texting-ship became. Jaden and I transitioned from innocent flirting to talking seriously about our potential relationship and what it could and would look like. Once I was in college, I wasn't really dating. I was still back and forth with Justin, but Jaden was my consistent source of attention and affection, although it was virtual. I became more attached to him.

At some point, we were saying "I love you" and talking about our potential future house and children. We were having phone sex almost every day. It was a little pathetic, really. I guess that's what happens after years of texting back and forth and making plans that would never actually happen. I think we were both comfortable with our delusions. I was busy with school and work and being social. Jaden was suffering from terrible anxiety that forced him to drop out of school, quit his job, and isolate almost all of his friends. We were there for each other, and we kept each other from being complete loners.

I used to genuinely believe that Jaden was one of the good ones. He always made me feel so good. He said such sweet things, he made me feel like I was one of a kind. I never blamed him for lacking the balls to see me in person. I believed him when he told me it was his anxiety, and he couldn't help it. Maybe that was true, but seeing him in a new light now, I doubt it.

A little over a year ago, I received a text from Jaden.

"I need to tell you something. I feel like you deserve to know, and I want you to hear it from me."

"Okay, sure. What's up?" I responded, quickly.

"I'm kind of seeing somebody."

Honestly, I wasn't upset. Like I said before, I had seen several other people while maintaining my texting-ship with Jaden. I was happy for him. He deserved to feel loved in real life. He deserved physical affection, I wanted that for him, and I told him that. I teased him a bit,

"You won't forget about me though, right? I can still text you and send you all of my most prized nudes?"

 I figured he would offer me the same decency I did him
for all of those years.

"Yeah, maybe."

 Maybe? What? Now I'm upset. I tell Jaden that of course
I'm happy for him, but he shouldn't forget who has been
there since day one. I've been a friend to him, haven't I? I
began to think that maybe I took Jaden for granted,
thinking he would always be around. But he told me he
would, he promised. And now, I was getting a maybe? I
had to know who the girl was that suddenly "cured" his
anxiety, allowing him to actually exist outside of a
screen. So, I asked. He was hesitant at first, but he told
me who it was. I said "Okay." and left it at that.

        Less than a year later, they are engaged. Now I'm
wondering if he ever really was one of the good ones. I
wonder if he tells her everything he used to tell me. I
wonder if he was only using me as a crutch until he felt
confident enough to enter reality again. I don't want to
believe these things. But a man that I used to think I
wanted to be with, or at the very least a man who would
be a lifelong friend, now refuses to speak to me. I made
efforts. I attempted to reach out in the most platonic way
possible. He shut me down, telling me he really just
wanted to focus on his new fiancé. I was disappointed, I

am disappointed. Clearly the bond I thought we shared was never a bond at all, but a convenience.

I hope it works out for him, because if it doesn't, who will he have? Not me.

Volume XII

Manuel

I thought very long and hard about whether or not I would talk about Manuel. Arguably the worst thing that has ever happened to me was at the hands of this man, if you can call him that. It's not an experience that is easy to relive, in fact, I am still not comfortable saying the words out loud. Before I begin, I would like to acknowledge that I know what this will look like. I am a white woman. Manuel is a Mexican man. Sharing this story can very well tarnish his name (if anyone finds out what his real name is.) I don't like that. It makes my stomach turn. I know how often white women cry "rape" against men of color, because they know they can. Because they know that men of color are viewed as predators in America, and white women so often feel the need to play victim. I feel guilty sharing this story because I don't want to feed into those dangerous stereotypes that leave many innocent black and brown men labeled as criminals. But on the other hand, I feel obligated to tell my truth. It feels necessary, like a part of the healing process, to share my experience. Before I go any further, I'd like to be clear that, just because this is what happened to me, does not make it the standard. Manuel is a different breed. All of his friends are entitled, rich, white men. (Refer to my feelings on these type of men on page 20.) I believe eventually this mentality rubbed off on him. I do not blame his race, I do not blame his family, I blame him and him alone. **Trigger Warning:** This is the story about the man who raped me.

Manuel and I started dating in the Summer. We are from the same town, and we were both home for the Summer. I was 19 years old, and so I felt too old to move back in with my parents. There wasn't much room for me anyways, I would have been sleeping on a couch and living out of a suitcase for three months. Instead I saved up some money to get myself a sublease on the U of I campus. Being from Champaign, growing up with a notorious party college as my backyard, the Summers were dedicated to going out with your friends. Somewhere in the midst of doing this, I met Manuel. I knew of him, but we had never actually talked. Turns out, he was very charming.

He would dazzle me with compliments and semi-corny pick-up lines. He would bring me food and flowers. He would show me off to his friends. He fit in well with my friends. This was all before we were even official. He was pulling out all of the stops to impress me. It was a little much, and a little fast, but how could I say no to that big smile that took up half of his face? It felt nice to be pursued so vigorously.

It didn't take long for Manuel and I to go Facebook official. We received a lot of attention as a couple. People seemed surprised, but happy for us. Shortly after the news leaked, Summer was over and it was time to go back to school in Chicago. Manuel and I were going to be in different cities, but they weren't too far from each other, and he had a car to visit when he could. We were enthusiastic, and confident that things would work out well between us. For the first couple of months, it did.

Manuel drove up to visit me almost every weekend. We texted all day, every day. Talked on the phone for hours at night. Sometimes I would take the train to him when he had soccer games and watch him in all of his glory. We saw each other plenty, it was never really an issue. Actually, our issues arouse for more unexpected reasons.

He was romantic. He believed in chivalry. The door was always held open for me, dinner was always paid for, flowers were never scarce. He wanted to hold hands at every waking minute, he wasn't afraid of PDA, and he was quick to tell me he loved me. It was as if Manuel's sole purpose in life was to make me happy. Sounds ideal, right? Only, it quickly became too much for me. In terms of types of love, I am not one to crave excess. So long as I have your honesty and attention, I don't need all of the extras. In fact, they make me a little uncomfortable. I don't really like being showered with niceties. It feels insincere, and I feel like I owe something in return. With that being said, I was emotionally

checked out of the relationship about a week before it
ended.

I never cheated on Manuel, but I did start
messaging Justin again. I talked with him about my
current relationship, and how I was thinking about
ending it. I told him that I was no longer attracted to
Manuel, and that I hated his friends and how he acted
around them. I shared with him the things that bothered
me most about my current relationship, and how it all
just felt very fake and trite to me. Justin, of course,
encouraged me to end things. He knew that if I did, we
would be able to fool around guilt free once again. (This
was before my big break off with Justin.) But really, I
didn't need much encouraging. I just wanted to wait for
the right time, I wanted to wait until he irritated me
again so that I could do it right there on the spot. I guess
I should have been very careful of what I wished for.

Manuel drove up to visit me on the weekend, and
he brought a friend. All of us, plus my roommate went
out for drinks and dancing that evening. My roommate
kept me company while the boys very obviously spent
their whole night trying to impress us. They pranced
around with their enormous egos, buying us shots and
trying to get us drunk enough to pay attention to them.
Anytime my roommate and I would disappear to the
bathroom or the bar, Manuel had a fit. I began to see just
how jealous and territorial he was. But honestly, I wasn't
in the mood to argue that night, so instead of ending

things right then and there, I kept it to myself and attempted to enjoy the rest of my night.

Once we were all danced out, we stumbled into the streets looking for a taxi to take us home. As soon as we got home, I wanted to take a shower. I set up a spot on the couch for Manuel's friend, and headed to my room for my robe and shower caddy. Manuel spent what felt like fifteen minutes trying to convince me to allow him in the shower with me. I said no every time, but he still followed me to the bathroom and began getting undressed. I think he noticed how frustrated I was getting when I looked at him seriously and said,

"I said no. Please get out. I just want to shower and go to bed."

He threw his hands up and left the bathroom.

I took a quick ten minute shower and headed back to my room. Turns out, ten minutes was all Manuel needed to rummage through every app on my phone. I walked in, and my phone was in his hand. He looked up at me with a face I had never seen before. My stomach dropped.

"Why do you have missed facetime calls from Justin?"

My heart sank. I didn't know how to respond. I hadn't cheated, and I did want to end things with Manuel, but for some reason I couldn't get myself to say that.

"We just had a conversation." I said, instead.

"What the fuck, Kira! What do you need to talk to him about? Why?!"

"We were just catching up."

A lie. But at this point the anger in his face was radiating and I spoke as soft as I could to keep him calm. My voice was apologetic, and slightly child-like,

"I'm sorry," I said, "I should have told you."

But Manuel was not in a forgiving mood. That big ego of his was hurt, and his pride told him he needed to lash out. So he yelled, and screamed, and called me names.

"YOU ACT LIKE A SLUT THEN YOU CRY WHEN YOU
GET TREATED LIKE ONE. YOU ARE A LIAR."

I was silent. I felt his spit hit my face as he screamed. I
heard my roommate knocking on the door, calling my
name. I ignored it, still frozen.

"I SHOULD HAVE FUCKING LISTENED TO MY
FRIENDS. THEY WARNED ME. THEY TOLD ME
JUSTIN WOULD BE A PROBLEM."

You're the problem. I thought. But I stayed silent. I lost
track of his words, eventually just focusing on his face. It
was bright red, every wrinkle in his forehead and chin
was revealed, and a thick blue vein emerged on his
forehead. Eventually I was backed into a corner of my
bed, when I reached out to grab his hands that were
whaling all around. This was my final effort to calm him.
He resisted immediately, throwing me off of him and
towards the wall. The side of my head bounced off of the
wall like a basketball, and tears finally streamed down
my face. I was no longer willing to apologize, or smooth
things over. There was not a single ounce of me that
wanted to be with Manuel anymore. Not a single piece of
me that was attracted, interested, or sorry for him. I
didn't care. I wanted him out, and I wanted to go to bed.

I thought about kicking him out, but we were both drunk, and I knew he couldn't drive. He had finally calmed down, and was laying down on my twin sized bed. I asked him to sleep on the floor, but he pretended to be too deep in his sleep to hear me. It was four in the morning, I had work in three hours. I decided it was time to accept my losses and try to get some sleep. I laid down next to him, attempting to take up as little space as possible. I made myself small so that our skin would not touch.

After sleeping for about an hour, I woke up to something strange. Our skin was touching again. The heat of his body was warming my flesh. I remember wanting to stretch out my legs, but they felt stuck. *Why?* I thought. I was in a daze, still feeling the liquor and lack of sleep. I realized my cotton shorts were pulled down to my knees. I blinked twice, and suddenly my head caught up with my body. That exact moment has stuck in the front of my mind like a parasite. It never goes away. The awakening. The understanding of what was happening. The moment in which I realized what was being taken from me.

I couldn't feel his warmth anymore. His body became needles against mine. His front was pressed against my back, and his hand was wrapped around my hip. He was using my body to hold himself in position. My body was now frozen, completely ice cold. I couldn't move my lips to say what I know I needed to. I wanted to scream at the top of my lungs. I wanted to cry, to tell him

"*NO.*" But I couldn't even open my mouth. I could barely open my eyes. My heart was beating so fast I could feel it in my throat, I could hear it in my ears.

I felt him trying to slide his parts into mine, but I was not ready. He was an intruder, my body did not want him. So he pushed himself inside of me, and I felt a sharp pain shoot from my cervix up through my spine. It felt like someone was rubbing sandpaper inside of me while sticking knives in my back. I remember listening to his murmured moans. He thought I was still asleep. I remember wanting to throw up. I remember feeling so heavy that I thought my body could crack open. I felt all of these things in a matter of two minutes before I finally found the strength to jump out of bed and pull my shorts back up to my waist. I jumped up so fast that I saw spots.

Manuel rolled back over, falling back asleep, as if nothing happened. I threw myself into the shower with scalding hot water and scrubbed myself raw. I felt so dirty. I washed my body three times before I got out. I remember telling myself to get it together, I had work in an hour, I needed to pull my shit together. I didn't have time to think about what had happened last night, or what may have happened five minutes ago. So I left for work, with the image of him still laying there, tainting my sheets, and his friend passed out peacefully on my couch. My entire apartment was silent, but I heard screams in my head.

I left for work, without saying a word to Manuel. When I came back, he was gone. We never spoke of what happened. We broke up through text message that evening.

I spent an entire year after, trying to figure out what it was that I was feeling. I knew something was very different, something felt very wrong. I hated looking at myself in the mirror. I was crawling in my own skin. My room didn't feel like my room, my clothes didn't feel like my clothes. I felt like a stranger to myself. My self-esteem was completely diminished.

Whenever I saw Manuel in public, my heart would race and my skin would tingle just like it did that night. When I saw pictures of my friends and him I thought about deleting every form of social media and disappearing from the world. I didn't understand why I felt the things I did, because Manuel didn't mean that much to me. I was never in love with him. Our relationship ended before it really began.

Manuel and I only dated for three months, but the aftermath of that night has been etched into my skin like a bad tattoo since. It took me a year to understand why. One day, in one of my sociology classes, we had a guest speaker. She passed out flyers to the entire classroom, stating facts, myths and statistics about rape. A few of them read,

Myth: Sexual assault is an act of passion. *Fact: Sexual assault is about power and control, used to punish or humiliate another person.*

Myth: If a rape victim does not fight back, they must have not thought the rape was that bad. *Fact: Many victims are in a state of shock, fear, or confusion about being raped.*

Myth: A person cannot sexually assault their partner. *Fact: 60% of rapes happen in the victim's own home, often times by someone they know. If a person does not consent to the sexual activity, it is rape.*

I felt like everything being described made way too much sense to me, it felt personal. It wasn't that these were things I didn't know to be true. I knew that rape was much more common than everyone thought, and I knew that it didn't always happen like it does in the movies; violently and in an alley. Nevertheless, the things I read on that flyer caused something to click with me. It all started to make sense. Everything I was feeling, everything I was afraid to say out loud. It hit me. The thought that was once a passing idea and was now reality to me, settled deep into my core. I was raped. By my boyfriend. My boyfriend raped me.

But understanding what happened to me was only the beginning. Even after I understood, I struggled with saying it out-loud. In fact, it took me a few more months to admit it to anyone. Eventually, I confided in a few close friends about that night and my real experience during and after. They were absolutely supportive, which made things easier of course. It felt good to get such a long-term heavy weight off of my chest. For a moment, I even felt empowered by saying the words out loud and calling out my ex for what he really was: A rapist.

I decided to come out and write a short story about that night. I entitled it *A Stranger in My Home* and posted it to my blog in which I often posted poems and rants. My blog didn't get much traffic, so I didn't expect any response. I was surprised when I started receiving messages from other young women, telling me that they were proud of me, and how important the story was for them. At least ten girls messaged me admitting that something similar had happened to them, but they were always nervous or hesitant about saying anything. It was a bittersweet feeling. It was nice to feel so supported, and as if something I did held meaning. But I was sad to know that what I went through, so many other girls were struggling with.

There was, of course, backlash as well. Although I didn't use his name in my story, a few of his friends made assumptions. Nobody said anything directly to me, but I was well aware that they talked amongst themselves, and to all of their acquaintances about how I was a liar and an attention-seeker. One girl, that Manuel had been lifelong friends with, saw me in a bar and tried to throw a drink on me. Two years later, she messaged me on Facebook and apologized. She said that she was sorry she didn't believe me, and now that something similar had happened to her, she felt terribly. I couldn't help but wonder if Manuel was her perpetrator as well.

It's possible that Manuel has tried to contact me, ask me about my story, accuse me of lying, accuse me of wanting it, or maybe even apologize. It's all possible. I wouldn't know. I blocked him out of my life completely the day after we broke up, and he will stay that way for the remainder of my life.

I was raped four years ago. I still have trouble saying the words out loud. One night, one moment, changed absolutely everything for me. It caused so much distress that I am still coping with. I used to hop from relationship to relationship, trusting so many careless men with my soul and my body. I never would have guessed one of them could have taken so much from me. I never even thought of rape by a significant other as a possibility. Until it happened. Now I'm here, picking up the pieces every day, while Manuel continues to live his life effortlessly.

Some days I look at my naked body in the mirror and wish I could literally crawl out of it. Some days I look at my boyfriend in fear and discomfort, holding him accountable for the entire male species. I do not hate men, but I am fearful of them. I am uncomfortable, mistrustful, and on edge around them. When I watch a scene in a movie or show that shows or talks about rape,

I get very emotional and irrational. My body reacts as if it's happening all over again. Sometimes, when my boyfriend and I have sex, I have flashbacks. I've never admitted that to him, or anyone for that matter. Sometimes I wonder if I'll ever be the fearless, unapologetic, sexual being that I once was. Sometimes I wonder if I'll ever forgive myself for failing to say "no." Sometimes I wonder if I'll ever genuinely trust another man again.

I am still so sad for myself, and for the parts of me that have been lost. A lot of that sadness has turned to rage, which I am grateful for. It makes me feel stronger. It reminds me of my purpose. To share my experiences, to be honest and raw with them, and to offer guidance and safety to any woman going through something similar. But, often times I am still sad, and scared. I spent an entire year feeling like I wanted to die and not understanding why. I'm so sad for the girl who couldn't explain the weight on her chest. I'm still hurting for the version of me who thought everyday about killing herself. I have come incredibly far, and I'm proud of that, but parts of that version of me is still very much alive.

I am hopeful that something good will come of this. I hope that someday, I will look back, and know that all of the torment was worth something. Someday, I will look within myself and acknowledge what I've survived. I will be able to say those words, I will be able to hear myself saying them, without reliving the moment. I will be able to speak and write openly about rape without losing my breath. Someday, something I've written will help a young woman through what she has endured. She will read my words, and they will resonate with her. They will be exactly what she needed, and they will help her become new. They will help her be whole again. I am hopeful. But I am also hurt.

Volume XIII

Aiden

After my experience with Manuel, I was extremely turned off by men. Most of them made me feel like I had the stomach flu. Summer was approaching again, and I got a new sublease on Campus. I was living on my own, working during the day, and going out with my friends at night. I had a brief situation with a girl named Hannah. Our friendship struck randomly, but fiercely. We did everything together. In fact, she ended up staying with me for a while after having a falling out with her parents. I know we were both attracted to each other, there was always a lustful tension when we were in a room alone. There were a couple of times that we kissed, and didn't talk about it after. There were a couple of times when I'd wake out of my sleep, and her body was wrapped around mine. We never really went there, although I wanted to.

Eventually Hannah and I had a falling out. I don't exactly remember why, but I do remember her being in a very messy and confusing place in her life. She was a bit of a tornado, causing destruction wherever she went. So we grew apart. And I was alone again.

I was okay with being alone. I liked it, even. My independence was much needed after my previous relationship. I needed to feel like my life was my own. I didn't love myself, but I wanted to and I was prepared to do the mental labor it took to get there. I wasn't looking for a relationship when I met Aiden, it just sort of happened.

That summer I was doing a lot of the drug popularly known as molly. I was grinding my teeth, having unnecessarily deep conversations with friends, and looking for anything to touch. One night, while I was riding my roll at a campus bar, I saw Aiden. He was the most adorable thing I'd ever seen in my life. He looked so sweet, innocent, and soft. I had seen him at house parties before, but never knew his name, and now I wanted to. I knew if I hadn't met him already, he probably wasn't the most popular guy. I was drawn to that. I was drawn to him because he was everything I wasn't.

After a little bit of liquid courage, I went straight up to him and introduced myself. I grabbed his hand, and started stroking it. I kept telling him how soft he was, in between asking him questions about himself and trying to catch my breath. He was so sweet and charming. He just smiled at me, and laughed, and answered all of my questions. He knew I was on something. He was a little tipsy, but not nearly as under the influence as I was. I later learned that Aiden was new to drinking and going out. He never smoked, never tried any drugs, and hardly got wasted. He was a late bloomer.

I could tell he had never come across a girl like me before. I could tell I made him nervous, and excited, and curious. I played into that. I liked the idea of being something new for him, a first for him. Something about switching the power levels, something about being the one with the control attracted me. I liked the idea of being someone he would never forget.

After our first encounter, I made him my mission. I asked one of his close friends, who ironically was trying to get with me, for Aiden's number. He reluctantly gave it to me, and I texted him that same night. We went back and forth for a while, and eventually agreed to hang out again sometime, while I was sober. We got very close, very quickly. I felt comfortable around him, and that held a new meaning for me being that my relationship prior was like walking on broken glass.

Despite the fact that we grew up very differently, I never felt like Aiden judged me. Not at first, at least. And we did grow up very differently. His family was well off. Their house was beautiful, I remember being so intimidated the first time he took me there. His mom is sweet and sophisticated, his dad is intense but funny, and his sister is quiet but beautiful. He grew up properly. With parents who loved each other and loved him. He was chubby as a kid, but his parents kept him in sports and made sure he maintained good grades. He had some insecurity issues because of the weight he used to have, but other than that he was pretty balanced.

I was quite the opposite. My family lived in a tiny house, where there is barely room to breathe. I don't talk to my father, my mother and I had just recently began rebuilding our relationships after her battle with opiate addiction. I came from a dysfunctionally dynamic home. I absolutely love the family I have, but we are messy. As for insecurities, I had my share. Who doesn't? However, the things I worry about are less physical and more about my mental state, or the lack of trust I've learned to have.

So here we were, completely opposite in every sense, but totally infatuated with each other. My sublease was ending, but he was moving into his apartment for the school year. He lived in Champaign full time, as a student. Once we became official, I was basically moved into his place. I had my own dresser drawer, and my own cabinet in the bathroom. Aiden had roommates, so our personal proximity was pretty much his room and bathroom. But still, it was nice.

Aiden felt like the type of guy I deserved. He felt like the type of guy I always avoided, because I thought I didn't. I felt like I finally found one of the good ones, but, there was one small catch. My sweet and practically straight-edge boyfriend.. was a virgin. I never really understood why. Yes, he had his insecurities. I mean, he barely let me see him without his shirt on, even though he was physically fit. But, he was good looking. Any girl could see that. He must have never really tried, because I can't imagine it would have been too difficult for him.

I didn't really mind the fact that he was a virgin. In fact, I think I liked it at first. I mean, to go from dating a rapist to a virgin. I had hit the jackpot. Of course, I didn't think about it this way in that moment. But, besides, I was plenty experienced for the both of us. And he didn't condemn me for that. I could show him what I liked, and how I liked it. This was my expectation. In reality, we had a lot of missionary sex with our shirts on. I wasn't as good of a teacher as I thought I would be. Sexually, I played more into the submissive role. Taking control was a challenge.

Our relationship was still good. Mediocre sex aside, Aiden was good to me. He was nice, he was honest, he was easy. I never had to worry with him. Summer was coming to an end, and I was running into some road bumps with school. I lost a lot of financial aid money and couldn't afford what I owed in order to register. My mom and I went over our options, and eventually I decided it best that I take the semester off. Although I was upset that I had to put my future on hold, I'll admit I was excited to get more time with Aiden. We were having fun. I would get to continue living responsibility free. Just working days, going out nights. I was living the life.

Aiden actually ended up being one of my longest standing relationships, at 8 months long. Impressive right? Looking back, I'm a little surprised we lasted as long as we did. The relationship was quiet and uneventful. I think I needed that though. I needed

someone I could just stand still with for a moment.
Someone who didn't come with drama, or baggage.
Someone who would just love me, and he did. Aiden
loved me. And I regret hurting him in the way that I did.
He genuinely did not deserve that.

Eventually, easy got boring to me. It wasn't
Aidens fault that I lost interest. I was just repeating a
pattern. Once I get set into a routine, I get anxious. I feel
stuck, and desperate to get out. I have always been like
this in relationships, I've never understood why. So here
I was, mentally detached from my relationship. Although
still sleeping in Aiden's bed every night. I was waiting for
an excuse to walk out of the door.

One Friday night, we decided we would go out. I
was getting ready, deciding what to wear when Aiden
walked in. I was trying on a white, cotton, button-up
shirt. I had the first three buttons undone, bearing a
little cleavage. It wasn't anything over the top, and I
thought I looked good. Aiden looked at me sideways for a
moment before saying,

"Why don't you button it up?"

Aiden had never commented on anything I had worn
before, at least not negatively. I was a little surprised.

"Why should I?" I responded defensively.

"I don't know, it's just a little low."

"No It's not. And who cares, anyways?"

"I just feel like you must want guys to hit on you if you wear that."

By this point, I was fuming. Had he no idea that he was saying something that goes completely against everything I believe in? I know that he never meant to upset me, and I know that he would have never done anything to hurt me. But that comment triggered me in ways that he could never understand. It felt like he was telling me that by wearing something semi-revealing, I deserved any harassment or assault that came my way. As dramatic as this sounds, it felt so real in that moment. But I didn't say anything. Visibly upset, I shut my mouth and changed my shirt.

I started cheating on Aiden a week later. Call it childish revenge, or my selfish way of getting out of the relationship. Whatever it was, Aiden didn't deserve it. I knew it all along, but it didn't stop me. I started texting back and forth with Justin again. We made plans to see each other. I started sleeping with a guy I worked with. Sex with him was everything but mediocre. I knew I didn't want to be with Aiden anymore, I just didn't know how to say it. I was being a coward. Spending less and less time with him, and more time sneaking around, when I should have just ended it.

I took a trip to Las Vegas with my best friend. We had a great time, but two hours before our flight home, we got a call with some bad news. A co-worker, and dear friend, of ours was dead. He died unexpectedly in a fire the night before. We could hardly believe it. He was so young, and such an amazing person, how could something like this happen? Nothing seemed to make sense. We cried the whole way home.

After this news, I gained a little clarity. Like, life is too short to be halfway in, halfway out. I knew I wanted out. I knew I needed to stop pretending. What was stopping me? I regret taking so long to break the news to Aiden. I regret my infidelity in the meantime. But what I regret the most, was how I ended it.

I sat at a bar with my best friend and vented. I went back and forth about how I was going to end it, what I would say, where I would do it. The more I thought about it, the worse I felt. I didn't want to face him. I didn't know how. After a few drinks, the same liquid courage that pushed me to approach Aiden the first night we met, was the same liquid courage that pushed me to break up with him... in a text message.

I prepared a novel in my iPhone notes. I started by explaining my recent distance that he may have noticed. I explained that our differences may have been more of a deal breaker than we thought it would be. I reassured him that he did nothing wrong. The good ol, "It's not you, it's me" speech. I apologized, a lot, for everything. I apologized for saying all of this in a text. I tried to explain that I knew when I saw his face, I wouldn't be able to say all of the things I wanted to say.

I let my best friend read over the note, and after her approval, I sent it and cringed. My stomach was tied into a hundred knots. The anticipation for his response was killing me, although it only took a few minutes. His response was short, and to the point.

"What do you want me to do with all of your stuff?" That was it.

"Throw it away." I responded. Then, right after, "I'm sorry."

That was it. There was no conversation after. He didn't give me an ounce of emotion, not that I deserved it, I was just surprised.

We still lived in the same town, went out to the same bars. There was a tension at first, but it faded. I wished good things for him. I hoped that he would learn to take the experiences I gave him, and use them elsewhere, use them on someone who actually deserved him. I hoped that I at least helped him step out of his comfort zone, so that he could go on to love someone who deserved it. I still have hopes that one day, we will have a real conversation. Face to face, talk about everything that happened and why it did. Maybe that's just my guilt weighing in, desperate to explain itself and be forgiven. But Aiden owes me nothing, and that's just something I've had to accept.

Volume XIV

Tony Part 1

After about 9 months in Champaign, I was ready to move back to Chicago. I was still working on getting my funds in order for school, and still not receiving any help to get back on track by financial aid, or anyone other than my mother for that matter. It was taking longer than I expected, and I knew that I didn't want to wait around in Champaign anymore. So I found a waitressing job, found an apartment, packed my things and moved.

My job was a wings spot on the south side. I liked it a lot. It stayed busy, so I was making good money, and I worked with a lot of people my age. I got along with pretty much everyone. About a month into working there, a new guy started in the kitchen. Apparently, he wasn't actually new, he was returning. But new to me, nonetheless. His sense of style caught my eye. He was part punk rocker, part skater boy, with a bit of a feminine side. He was skinny and only a few inches taller than me. He wore one hoop earring, and a braided mullet. He was the most interesting man I'd ever encountered. Nothing like I'd ever known, and insanely attractive to me. The way he moved and talked was so relaxed and unapologetic. The way he smiled was so

young and genuine. His hands looked like hard work. I
wanted to know everything about him.

I asked around. People at work told me that his
name was Tony, and he's a great guy. However, he had
just gotten out of a really weird and long relationship
and had sworn off white women. I didn't blame him, we
can be very problematic. According to everyone else, it
wasn't worth trying. I wouldn't be his type. That made
sense, he was much more eclectic than I. A couple of
people even tried to convince me that he was gay. It was
clear nobody thought I had a chance, so I brushed it off
and swooned from a distance.

About a week later, Tony shouted at me from the
kitchen window, "Hey, you never followed me back on
Instagram."

"Huh?" was my immediate response.

"Yeah, I followed you." He insisted. I looked at my
notifications.

"Oh wait, yeah. My avitar is an anime character." He
mentioned, laughing.

Sure enough, there he was. I followed him back, and smiled.

"There you go." I said.

That night after work, he messaged me on the app.

"Do you want to hang out sometime?" It read.

My stomach turned into a mixture of mush and butterflies. Did he know I was into him? Did somebody tell him?

"Yeah, forsure. When are you free?" I replied, probably way too fast.

We hung out the following week. I was nervous, and considered cancelling, but decided I'd have to face him at work anyways. I contemplated what to wear. We were just going to hang out at my house for a bit, maybe grab some diner food. I didn't want to look like I was trying too hard, so I threw on some Calvin Klein grey sweatpants that made my ass look phenomenal, and a cropped zip up. Comfortable, but cute.

When Tony showed up, we just sat at my kitchen table for a while and talked. It was strange. We sat across from each other, so formal like, as if we were in an interview. But the conversation flowed so naturally. We went from discussing our days, to our jobs, to music, to the social injustices of the world. We talked as if we had known each other forever. I could have talked to him all night.

We decided to take a break from the deep conversations and grab some food with some of our other co-workers. A friend picked us up, and we headed to a 24/7 diner nearby. Afterwards, around 2 in the morning, we were both dropped back off at my house. Tony lived less than a mile from me, so I assumed he would walk home. Without even asking, I hugged him before going back up to my apartment.

"Let's hang out again, soon. I'll text you." I said.

He looked a little caught off guard. He hesitated before agreeing, and then took off. It took me a moment to realize, but he must have thought he was going to stay the night.

A couple of days later, we hung out again. We both had the day off of work, so he came over in the middle of the afternoon. I remember being thrown off by his outfit. As I mentioned before, I had already noticed that he had a bit of a softer and feminine side. But it usually wasn't more than an earring or painted nails. He came over wearing a cropped and tight-fit velvet shirt, a choker necklace, and his usual accessories.

Now mind you, I've always been one to reject gender roles, and I'm fully aware that a person's outfit does not directly correlate to their sexual identity. I wasn't bothered, nor was I turned off. I was just a little surprised. I had never found myself attracted to someone like Tony before. But here I was, so eager to find out if he was attracted to me, as well. I studied his face, and the tone in his voice. I listened carefully to the things he said, just hoping to figure him out.

We were sitting on my couch, far apart enough that we weren't touching, but close enough to feel flirtatious. We were talking about pop culture and music, and I asked him if he liked Frank Ocean. He had just come out with the album *Blonde* that I was listening to every day.

"Hell yeah. I love Frank Ocean, he is like.. He's crazy. He's so cute." Tony responded in such excitement.

Cute? Now I was even more confused. Was Tony into guys? Were the people at work right? Did I even care? I knew he had recently broken up with his girlfriend, so he had to be into girls, too. I tried to act natural and keep the confusion from showing up on my face. But as soon as he left, I did some serious internet digging.

I found pictures of him, his friends, and yes, his ex-girlfriend. She was pretty, but very opposite from me. She had black hair and pale skin. She wore thick eyeliner and band t-shirts. After doing my research, I came to the conclusion that there was no way Tony was into me. There was no way that I was his type. He was an art kid, who went to punk shows, and had a million friends who were all creative and experimental and a little weird. His life seemed way cooler than mine. We were just going to be friends, and that was fine.

The third time we hung out felt more relaxed. My nerves eased up a bit, and I started to feel more comfortable. He must have felt the same, because after watching a movie together he turned to me and asked,

"Would it be cool if I stay over tonight?"

"Yeah, for sure." I responded, very nonchalant.

Although my insides were full of question marks. I could not figure this kid out. I had absolutely no idea if he was into me, but I seriously doubted it. So what, did he just want to crash on my couch? And for what? What was he about, what was going on in his head, in his life, I felt desperate to know.

To my surprise, he ended up sleeping in my bed, with me. I offered him some sweatpants so he would be more comfortable. We laid side by side, in my creaky bed. We listened to Frank Ocean's *Blonde* and began to doze off. I turned to my side and was pleasantly startled with Tony pulled me closer to him. For such a skinny guy, he felt so strong and sure of himself against my skin. His body heat melted into me, while his overworked hands rubbed firmly all around my body. I remember falling in love with those hands, and the way they felt against me that night.

Eventually he turned me around, and began kissing me. He looked at me seriously for a moment,

"Is this okay? Do you want to have sex?" He asked.

This was the first time a man had ever actually asked for my consent. Strangely, it made me a little uncomfortable. It was something I wasn't used to, and had no experience reacting to. So I rolled my eyes and told him to shut up.

"Some things go without saying." I told him, and kissed him harder.

And we did, have sex, on the third night. And it was so good. Genuinely the best I had ever had. I was so surprised that a man who was skinnier than me, not much taller than me, and almost as feminine as me could make me feel that way. My whole body craved more. I was hooked. I was sold.

It wasn't so simple for Tony, though. I later learned that he was much more hesitant than I. He was quick to get physically close to me, but emotionally he needed a little bit of guidance and a whole lot of patience. I was willing to dish it out for a while. Tony gave me the rundown on his past relationship, and it was clear that he wasn't ready for a new one. So, we continued hanging out, and having sex, but seeing other people. We kept it casual, and for a while, I was fine with this. For a while it was fun.

But after a few months, fun turned to messy. I was hardly interested in any of the other people I was seeing. I was only giving them attention to prove a point to Tony. I wanted to make him jealous. I wanted him to realize how desired I was, and how lucky he was to be the one I wanted. But in reality, nobody made me feel the way that he did. Things with Tony felt new and exciting. I knew that I had fallen for him. I knew what I wanted, and I expressed my feelings, hoping that he would reciprocate them. But he just wasn't at that point. He was willing to agree on seeing each other solely, because he wasn't seeing much of anyone else to begin with. It was the whole "boyfriend and girlfriend" idea that turned him off. I couldn't completely wrap my head around why he was so against it. He preached about the idea of monogamy being unnatural and a scam, and I was intrigued by his ideals but I also just wanted to be with him.

I was getting impatient. I was considering the pro's and con's of moving on.

Pro's: We don't want the same thing. I can pretend to want it, but I know I want more. I can focus on myself. Relationships are messy and distracting. I can have sex with whoever, whenever I want. I'm free.

Con's: I love him. He's become my best friend.

So, still on the edge, I planned events for my upcoming birthday. I wanted to take a trip, and I was making decent money at work. So my roommate and I planned a long weekend getaway to Puerto Rico. It was everything I needed. Sun, sand, drinks, great food. I loved it. I didn't want to leave, but I missed my hard headed lover back home. This was the longest I had gone without seeing him since we met. I was ready to get home and kiss him all over.

Only when I got home, there was some irritating news waiting for me. Some of my friends from work informed me that while I was gone, Tony was sneaking around with one of the new girls. Apparently, they had been having private conversations in the back of the restaurant. One of my co-workers even mentioned seeing Tony in this new girls snapchat story, at her house. I was fuming. Why didn't he tell me? I was more upset at the fact that he had failed to mention it than the fact that he actually did it.

I was prepared to give him the benefit of the doubt. So I confronted him about it. I asked him to explain himself, and to just be honest about what happened. He seemed annoyed. He was very upset that people were telling me these things. I didn't know if it was because they weren't true, or because he didn't want me to know. He rambled about how it was nothing, there were no secret conversations. They were just friends, talking at work. Nothing happened. He wasn't trying to hide anything.

Okay. I thought. Then why didn't you tell me? And I knew he still wasn't telling me the full story.

"So you never went to her house?"

"Oh yeah, but only for an hour."

Oh yeah? I thought, probably out loud. How do you forget to mention that you went to her house?

"Why were you there?"

"We stopped by there before we went out."

HA. OH. "So, you went out together?"

"Yeah?"

I couldn't believe how careless he seemed about the situation. He couldn't believe I was upset. We were getting nowhere. Looking back, I know the situation was ridiculous. But I felt like a fool. Here was this man, that I was head over heels for. A man that I wanted a relationship out of, and everyone knew it. Meanwhile, he is going out with other girls that we work with, without even mentioning it. I have to hear it from everyone else. I felt stupid, and it was enough to push me away. It was the reminder that we are just not on the same page that I needed to walk away.

I took a day to myself to think it over and think of what to say. I listened to break-up songs, hoping to encourage myself to end this situationship. Lord knows I had enough of those for one lifetime. When I was ready, I walked over to his house. It felt like the longest 6 blocks ever. The anticipation was lodged in my throat. When I finally got there, we went into his bedroom and I sat on the floor. I was silent for a moment, and he waited patiently.

Eventually I let out my long, rehearsed, run-on sentence filled monologue.

"I believe you when you say nothing happened but that doesn't change the fact that you didn't tell me in the first place and that makes me feel like you have something to hide. I don't want to feel like I'm constantly searching for the truth from you, or forcing it out of you. I don't want to feel like I have to convince you not to mess with other people. I spent a lot of time chasing after a boy who didn't want the same things as me and I can't do that with you. I know what I want and if you don't then I can't do this. You can't just string me along. I know you don't mean to but it feels toxic." I continued rambling for a solid fifteen minutes, but was stopped in my tracks when I heard

"Okay. I'll give you what you want, then."

...

"What do you mean?"

"I'll be with you."

"Well not if you don't want to. I don't want to force you to do anything."

"I mean, it's not what I originally wanted, but if it means not losing you."

I just looked at him, confused. Yes, this is what I wanted but, it felt wrong. It felt forced. But this was the first time he expressed any fear of losing me, and I have to admit, it felt good to be wanted.

"Are you sure?" I asked, skeptically.

"I'm sure of one thing, and I know my feelings for you. They were unexpected but they are definitely there. I don't know if a relationship will work but I'm down to try it if it's what you need from me."

That's it? I thought. *That's all it took to change your mind?*

I was still skeptical, but relieved, and a little guilty about feeling so excited.

"Okay then. We're together. You're my boyfriend. Ew, weird." I laughed.

We didn't jump to tell anyone, and we didn't document it on social media. Things moved pretty slow at first. Honestly, I was afraid he would change his mind. We both carried our doubts over to the other side. I wasn't sure at first, but I felt like he resented me a little. I felt like he wasn't happy. So I treaded lightly, not expecting too much, and staying on my toes.

I knew Tony loved me, we had already shared those words, unconventionally in the midst of an argument, of course. I knew he didn't want to lose me, he had made that clear. I knew he was willing to make sacrifices and test his comfort for me. I think that he knew it too, and he hated it. I think he resented me for making him care about anything.

About six months into our relationship, things took a turn. For some reason I had a gut feeling that something was off. If I have learned anything, it's to always trust my instincts in relationships, they rarely steer me wrong. So I did a little digging, hoping to ease my mind. I went through Tony's laptop, looking at his Facebook and Twitter messages. I didn't find anything deeming him unfit for a relationship, or unhappy with the one we were in. But there was one girl that caught my eye. The way she spoke to him came off a little strange to me, a little too comfortable.

I thought of ways to bring it up to Tony without admitting I had rummaged through his messages. I knew it would cause an argument, I knew he'd be upset, and naturally I wanted to avoid that. He came over after work that night.

"Hey, can we talk about something?" I asked.

He looked at me, a little nervous.

"Yeah? Everything OK?"

"Yeah yeah. It's nothing too serious, just a conversation I think we should have."

My goal was to make Tony comfortable with telling me anything. I wanted him to know that if there was something going on, it would be better to be honest. I explained that we had been together for half of a year, and things were going good. I told him how happy I was, and how proud I was of him. I admitted that I had my doubts, and that moving forward I wanted to be at ease. Moving forward I wanted to be open books.

"Even if you think it might hurt my feelings. Just tell me how you feel. Tell me what's going on in your mind. I need to know. We need to talk about these things so that we can grow together."

I could see the debate in his face.

"If there's anything in the past. If there is anybody I should be worried about. If anything weird has gone on, I expect you to tell me yourself. I will find out one way or another. I always do." I looked at him seriously, but softly.

At this point, I could tell by the look in his face there was something I needed to know.

"Okay. Don't get mad, but there is something. It was like three months ago. And I didn't cheat or anything. But I was at this party back in my hometown. I got really drunk, we were all really drunk. I passed out on the couch, and this girl laid on the floor right next to the couch. She started touching me, and I kind of started touching her back."

My tone changed, much less soft this time.

"What do you mean, how?" I urged.

"Like, in each others pants. But it was super quick, and I immediately regretted it and stopped. Nothing else happened."

"You don't consider that cheating?" I snapped, very hard this time. "Your hands were in another girls pants! Are you kidding me?"

His face went bright red. I don't think he understood to what extent this would hurt me.

"I'm sorry. I didn't think it was. I was mad, we were fighting. I wanted to get back at you. I wanted to prove that I didn't deserve you. Like I wanted to prove to myself I couldn't really be in a relationship."

My eyes flooded and my stomach turned. I felt sick, completely disgusted.

I cried myself to sleep that night. I woke up crying the next morning. I couldn't get out of bed. My body felt stuck while my mind was pacing back and forth between my options. *I should leave him, right?* I thought. *That's what you're supposed to do in these situations. That's what strong women do.* But I looked at him, crying too, begging me to get out of bed. I felt myself feeling more sorry for him than I did myself. I felt myself wanting to take care of him, make him feel better. And that made me even more angry. I felt like my love for him robbed me of my right to be angry. I didn't get the chance to be hurt because I was too busy wanting him to be happy.

I never thought of myself as a very forgiving woman. Priding myself on my independence and my feminist beliefs, how could I stay with a man who had been unfaithful? I saw myself in Tony. I saw the anguish in his mistakes. I've seen a lot of bull and heard a lot of shit. I like to think I'm fairly good at separating that from what is genuine. I believed Tony when he apologized. I knew that he wanted to hurt himself more than he wanted to hurt me.

I forgave him. I told him that I needed space, and I needed him to be patient with me during the process, but that I could forgive this. He agreed. He promised me it would never happen again, assured me it genuinely meant nothing. It didn't make me feel better about it, but the regret in his face gave me some peace. I told myself that this must be my karma, for the other guys I cheated on with Justin. Maybe this was the universe making things right. I told myself that if it happened again, that was it, I was out. Although, if we're being honest, I'm still not sure if that's true. I surprise myself with what I'm willing to get over.

Tony did a 180 after that night. He was everything I needed him to be. He was everything I was hoping for from the start. The fear of losing me forced a change in him, and I have to admit that was satisfying for me. I felt like for the first chapter of our relationship I was the desperate one, spreading myself thin to make it work. I was so in love with the person he was, I believed in him. So I broke some of my rules, and morphed some of my shapes to fit into his life. Now, he was doing so for me.

On his best behavior, I was Tony's first priority. All of his free time, attention, love was dedicated to me. It was nice for a while. But honestly, it wasn't all necessary. All I needed from Tony was his honesty, respect, and reciprocity. We learned to give each other what we needed, and never take too much. We found a balance, and it's been right ever since.

Yes, Tony and I are still together. For just a moment, I stopped listening to how everyone else told me to feel. I stopped following everyone else's rules, and I did what I wanted to do. And that's not to say I did the right thing, but I absolutely did what felt right to me. I'm not preaching or suggesting that women should forgive their cheating boyfriends or husbands. Maybe I made the weak decision and chose to remain blinded by the love I had rather than exercise my strength. Or maybe I made the strong decision, and pushed myself to a level of forgiveness that challenged my core values for a person I still loved and respected. Or maybe I just made a decision, a decision that I'm happy with currently. And maybe that's okay, and maybe it's nobody else's business.

Anyways, we have been together for almost two years now, and that drunken night is no longer even a blimp on our radar. We just signed our first lease together, and we move in at the end of this month. I'm incredibly excited to start this chapter together. This has been my first real, adult relationship where I have seen myself and my partner grow thanks to each other. This has been my most sincere connection with another human being, in which I feel comfortable enough to share all of my embarrassing and sometimes scary thoughts. And this has been the first love that I have had that isn't out of manipulation, or toxic patterns.

Tony Part 2

A lot has changed since I finished the first version of Tony's chapter. I considered deleting it all together and starting over. However, I wanted this collection of stories to be as genuine as possible, so why get rid of the original truth? It still stands, it's still relevant, so let's all be real here.

Two weeks after finishing the chapter, and a week before moving into our new apartment, Tony and I came to a very big fork in the road of our relationship. Let me start from the beginning.

Tony went out with some friends after work one night. It was getting late and he wasn't answering my calls or texts. I started to get anxious, when he finally picked up the phone and answered with a sharp tone,

"What, Kira?"

"Tony? Are you okay?"

"Yes, I just can't do this."

"What are you talking about?"

"I think you know exactly what I'm talking about. I'm leaving."

"Tony, I seriously have no idea what's going on. Please come over so we can talk about this."

"Fine, I'm on my way."

My stomach was in knots, my heart was racing. I couldn't sit still, I couldn't stop crying. I was so confused, and nervous and upset. Tony finally got to my house at 2 in the morning. He seemed to have calmed down a bit, but I was shaking. We sat on my porch and didn't move until 5 hours later.

Tony admitted that he was having some serious issues with our relationship. He didn't feel comfortable talking to me, anymore. He felt judged and stuck. He felt like I didn't actually like him, I only liked the version of him I had created in my head. He insisted on leaving, saying that he wanted to move to New York and start over. He said that there was nothing keeping him in Chicago and he just couldn't stay here anymore. And to put the final nail in the coffin, he admitted to having feelings for someone else. One of his best friends, whom I had always been suspicious of, but was always told not to worry about. A girl who I had tried to befriend at one point but ended up despising down the road. A girl who was my complete opposite. A girl who also lives in New York, and I was certain put these ideas in his head. This was the hardest nail to swallow. It still hasn't quite gone down.

I was soaking up all of this information, unsure of how to react. All I could do was cry, and sob, and plead, and so I did. I cried so much that I couldn't see straight.

"Please, don't do this to me. You can't just leave me like this. You can't fuck me over on this lease, a week before. You can't fuck me over on this relationship, 2 years later. You just can't." I pleaded through my tears.

I just couldn't fathom that this was real. This was not my reality. That level of rejection, disrespect and loss was too much for me to take in. I was hysterical for hours.

After finally calming down, and realizing the sun had come up, we decided to go to bed, and talk more in the morning. I didn't actually fall asleep, and about an hour later, Tony woke up too.

"I'm starting to regret everything I said. I don't really know what to do, or think right now." he said, hesitantly.

His words instilled a sense of hope in me. Maybe there was a chance to save this relationship. I treaded lightly, trying to pick his brain, trying to figure out where his head was. We ended up having the most open, honest, understanding and revealing conversation of our entire relationship that morning. We laid it all out there; the good, the bad, and the ugly. We listened to each other, we didn't judge and we didn't condemn. We showed each other support and love, and we ended up coming to an agreement.

I assured Tony that I was not upset about him having feelings for somebody else. I myself, am a firm believer in the possibility of loving two people at once. I admitted to him that I have never gotten over Justin, and I still kept in contact with him from time to time. I explained to Tony that what truly upset me was the fact that he was so ready to walk away from everything. I wanted him to feel comfortable talking to me about things, instead of reacting irrationally and self-destructing. I reminded him that what he does affects me, whether he wants it to or not. And that, even though I could understand where he was coming from, I was hurt. I couldn't help but feel betrayed and humiliated. I couldn't help but see myself as a burden, as some girl who he just didn't love enough, as some girl he was willing to toss to the side like it was nothing. I also reminded him of my mistrust in the other woman he developed feelings for.

"You can't help who you fall for, I get that. But her? Really? She is such an evil person. So manipulative, so selfish, so ugly inside."

 I hated her. I felt like she did this intentionally. I felt like she found Tony in a weak, and vulnerable state, and took advantage.

"Just be careful," I continued, "I see her for what she is, and I know you're blinded by what you want her to be. So just be careful."

        Without blaming me for the way I felt, Tony assured me that he didn't love me any less than he always has. He told me that he felt a lot better about our relationship knowing that he could open up without being judged or hated. He went back and forth, frustrated, confused, and visibly overwhelmed, repeating that he didn't know what to do; he didn't know what the right thing to do was. It felt good to hear that he did still want to be with me, but he knew something had to change, and I knew it too. We just could not stay stuck in this rut, distracted by routines and holding in our true feelings, even if they were towards other people.

"Whatever you decide, know that I love you. Know that I have been blessed to know you. Know that I will be here no matter what, and I am willing to work on this if you are." I assured him, trying to end the conversation on a positive and hopeful note.

I racked my brain trying to decide if *I* was doing the right thing. Was I being a complete idiot? Should I have spit in his face, and let him leave? Was I getting myself into a complete, pathetic mess? I considered every option, but ultimately, I knew what felt right, and I went with that. I could lie to myself all I wanted, but I knew that my ways of loving someone were toxic. My idea of love has always been laced with control, jealousy, and possessive tendencies. I was attached to the thought that love was supposed to look like a romantic comedy. I was so invested in my hopeless romantic dreams that I forgot what was really important, and I forgot to pay attention to my real needs and those of my lover.

So now, it was time for me to sit down and have an honest conversation with myself. What was I feeling, and why? What do I really require in a relationship, and what are things I ask for out of insecurities? How can I make my love more honest and genuine? I came to a realization that monogamy was not as important to me as it once was, or as I once thought it was. It was a pretty thought, two people, in love and willing to cut off the world for that love. Pretty, but unrealistic. I acknowledged that it would take me a considerable amount of time to get over this, and that the beginning would be a difficult adjustment, but that ultimately, I could. I could get over this.

Tony seemed surprised when I shared this news with him. He expected that I'd hate him forever and want nothing more to do with him. But I was here to stay. I was still in love with him, I was still excited to live with him and grow with him, and if he said that he felt the same way, why give that up so easily? We gave it a couple of weeks to settle in before revisiting the terms of our relationship. I will not sugar coat it, it was a rough couple of weeks. Between the stress of moving in to a new place, and the uncertainty of my relationship in the air, I was on edge. I was not sleeping or eating, I was barely speaking for that matter. My head was in a weird state of limbo, not quite ready to accept everything. And my heart was completely broken. It felt like I was going through a break up with the man I was moving in with. I didn't know how to feel or how to behave, so I just sort of shut down.

While some of these mixed and complicated emotions are still present, things definitely got easier after we had *the talk*. We needed to set boundaries, establish trust and understanding. It was less about labeling the relationship, and more about talking about what works for us. I knew that monogamy was out of the picture, and while I was still mourning the relationship that once was, I wasn't necessarily against that. As you guys know now, I've cheated in pretty much every relationship I've been in, so maybe trying something different was long overdue.

As far as boundaries go, we agreed to keep things separate and safe. We agreed that our home is our safe place. When we are here, we are present and considerate. Above all, we wanted to be as nice to each other in the process as possible. We acknowledged that this transition would not be easy, but as long as we are respectful, and as long as the love remains, we could make it work. I'm no expert in the art of open relationships, but I felt like we were doing an OK job so far. I felt like we were being proactive and mature, and that gave me a sense of ease.

It's been about a month into our new found "open relationship." As far as Tony's outside romance goes, I do not want to share too much, as it is not my business necessarily to share, and I'd like to respect at least an ounce of his privacy. However, I will say that my concerns and warnings were appropriate. Yes, I was right. She did not turn out to be who Tony hoped she would, and now he is dealing with the hurt of that. I am trying to be as supportive as possible, and to avoid the ever so deserved "I told you so." I am sure he will find someone new, and I'm encouraging him to play the field. I'm a bit apprehensive, as the last time he found himself swooning over another, he did not handle it with grace and care. I have asked him from here on out, to give me the respect that I deserve. I have made it clear that I expect a certain level of appreciation, I feel as though, especially now, it is owed to me. I have done my own share of playing the field a bit. It's turned out to be a rather refreshing experience, actually.

I am learning how dynamic human beings are. I feel as though we are completely capable, maybe even meant to have multiple loves. Sometimes I imagine myself with love filling every corner of my body up that it spills out and into others. I love love. I love being in love, I love being loved. I love new love, I love old love, I love familiar love and I love a love that tests me. Connections and experiences are so important, and the idea of that is what makes this okay for me. If I want that for myself, I cannot be upset with Tony for having that same desire. And whatever connection I develop outside of my relationship with him does not take away from the love we have manifested. There is no way it ever could. That is a love that is planted very deep. It's a love that I cannot hide from or tuck away. It is a love that I am proud of, protective of, and still very much invested in.

And when you love someone in that way, shouldn't you want the best for them? If you truly love them, as the person they are, not the person you want them to be, wouldn't you want them to feel free and active in life? Wouldn't you want to see them grow, to learn new things, to exist- like really, intentionally, exist in the world? If these are things we want for ourselves, shouldn't we want them for our lovers? Like I said before, I am no expert in all that is open relationships, I'm figuring it out as I go, so my logic may be completely flawed. But these are things I tell myself, and they have

.ispire me. I want to learn how to love
.ıy without needing to feel like they belong to me,
.se that is how I want to be loved. I want to love in a
that sets me free.

. am confident that if I continue to work past the hate
and the insecurity that I have been taught to hold onto,
and focus on the things that I really require, and the love
that I have, good things will come to me. Good things
will come to my dearest lover. Good things are coming.

Volume XV

Me

I grew up watching romantic comedies and singing along to slow, sad, sappy songs. I yearned for the type of love that people write entire novels about. Ever since my first kiss, I daydreamed about a love that would consume me. I hoped that one day, someone would love me so much that they would do anything to prove it. *Sacrifice,* I thought, is how someone proves they love you.

I grew up watching my mother treat relationships like they were disposable objects, jumping from man to man. I heard her scream, watched her cry, rinse and repeat. My mother had a sharp tongue and she was never afraid to use it. She wasn't afraid to hurt anyone's feelings, she wasn't afraid of loss. In fact, she acted as though she welcomed it, encouraged it even. I think this was her way of keeping people at an arm's length. I always thought it was just because she was so independent, and I admired that in her. I mimicked her behaviors and became a distorted version of her.

I grew up watching my father disappear. I watched him build a life for himself, start a new family, one that didn't include me. He would come around every once in a while, offering empty promises and excuses. He

me why I never called him, as if I was the
nen I told him I missed him, and wanted him
d more, he would swear to do better. As I got older,
gan to realize it just wasn't going to happen. I also
egan to realize, I didn't really want it to. My father is
not a good man. He has made racist comments about my
half black little brother. He has made inappropriate
comments about the way I choose to dress. Once, after
going almost an entire year without reaching out to me,
he tried to hit on my best friend via Facebook. I grew up
tolerating my fathers disrespect; the only thing that he
was consistent in. I allowed him to manipulate me, and
despite all of the pain he caused while doing so, I still
feel obligated to love him.

I suppose it all comes full circle. The way my
parents loved me, loved each other, loved themselves, or
didn't; that love, or lack thereof, planted the seed. It was
up to me to let that seed grow into something new and
strong, or let it fester into something old and sad. It
festered for a while. I loved like my mother; a little
tough, never fully, and usually short-lived. I accepted
love like my fathers; wishy-washy, immature, and
selfish. This was my idea of love for a while. I didn't
know anything else.

Naturally, as I grew older, I started developing
some habits of my own. I have had my own experiences;
some good, some bad, some damaging and life-altering
experiences. Although some of them were unfortunate,
one in particular still sits like an illness in me, I have

been able to move forward, always. I am becoming the woman I am supposed to be. I am discovering my desires, my fears, my needs, my insecurities, my soul. Here I am, almost 24 years old, slowly learning how to love and navigate romantic relationships on my own terms.

Everyone has their own path. Everyone has their own version and ideas of love, and that's okay. There is no right or wrong answer. There is only emotion and truth. Like I mentioned in the very beginning of this book, love is the most universal craving in the world. It connects us all, as every child is born needing it and every elder dies clinging to it. It sits at the center of every being. I am no one special. My stories are no more important, my experiences are no more valid than anyone else's. But I do see a beauty in the connection of all of my lovers and losses. I do see a beauty in the consequences and the results. After it all, there is me. There will always be me, and there is no better feeling than knowing that is enough. There is something special about falling in love with yourself.